Praise for *Letters to a Young Therapist*

"In *Letters*, Pipher comes across as more of a tribal elder than clinician, an empathetic observer offering solid advice that just happens to be supported by decades of research and experience."
—*Florida Times-Union*

"Pipher's book just might be one of the most soothing books you'll ever read."
—*The Plain Dealer*

"*Letters to a Young Therapist* is upbeat. It sees life's proverbial cup as half full."
—*Lincoln Journal Star*

"(G)iving advice seems to be second nature to her."
—*Kirkus Reviews*

"Refreshing, informative and insightful."
—*Publishers Weekly*

"Mary Pipher is a national treasure. Everyone, not just therapists, can benefit from this wise, compassionate, lovely book."
—Jean Kilbourne, author of *Can't Buy My Love*

"Writing with her usual grace, compassion and humility, Pipher once again proves herself to be a magnificent storyteller and a wise, trustworthy guide for our times. She speaks straight to the heart."
—Harriet Lerner, Ph.D., author of *The Dance of Anger*

letters to a
young therapist

The Art of Mentoring from Basic Books

Letters to a Young Lawyer
Alan Dershowitz

Letters to a Young Contrarian
Christopher Hitchens

Letters to a Young Golfer
Bob Duval

Letters to a Young Conservative
Dinesh D'Souza

Letters to a Young Activist
Todd Gitlin

Letters to a Young Therapist
Mary Pipher

Letters to a Young Chef
Daniel Boulud

Letters to a Young Gymnast
Nadia Comaneci

Letters to a Young Catholic
George Weigel

Letters to a Young Actor
Robert Brustein

Also by Mary Pipher

The Middle of Everywhere:
The World's Refugees Come to Our Town

Another Country:
Navigating the Emotional Terrain of Our Elders

The Shelter of Each Other:
Rebuilding Our Families

Reviving Ophelia:
Saving the Selves of Adolescent Girls

Hunger Pains:
The Modern Woman's Tragic Quest for Thinness

Mary Pipher

letters to a
young therapist

stories of hope and healing

BASIC
BOOKS

A Member of the Perseus Books Group
New York

The names and identifying details of all clients have been changed to protect confidentiality.

Copyright © 2003 by Mary Pipher

Paperback edition published in 2005
Hardcover edition published in 2003

Published by Basic Books,
A Member of the Perseus Books Group

Books published by Basic Books are available at special discounts for bulk purchases in the United States by corporations, institutions, and other organizations. For more information, please contact the Special Markets Department at the Perseus Books Group, 11 Cambridge Center, Cambridge, MA 02142, or special.markets@perseusbooks.com.

Library of Congress Cataloging-in-Publication Data
Pipher, Mary Bray.
  Letters to a young therapist: stories of hope and healing / Mary Pipher.
    p. cm.
  ISBN 0-465-05766-7 (hardcover)
  1. Psychotherapy—Miscellanea. I. Title.
  RC480.5.P544 2003
  616.89'14—dc21
                                    2003003603
  ISBN 0-465-05767-5 (paperback)

05 06 07 / 10 9 8 7 6 5 4 3 2 1

Dedicated to
Jim Pipher and Jan Zegers,
my lifelong office mates

■ Contents

PART III: SUMMER

PART IV: FALL

Acknowledgments

Thanks to Jamie Pipher, my first reader, and to Sara Pipher, my last one.

Also to readers Pam Barger, Lynda Madison, Jim Pipher, and Jan Zegers

Thanks to John Lehnhoff, who was our office mate for a time and to my writer's group, Prairie Trout.

To mentors and friends in the mental health field—Hank Balters, Francis Baty, Lynette Smith Causey, Eli Chesen, Jim Cole, Dru Copeland, Dick Dienstbier, Laura Freeman, Marcia Freer, Bill Doherty, Carmen Grant, Ken Gregoire, George Hachiya, George Hanigan, Dave Hansen, Herb Howe, Mary Kenning, Carol Lowery, Frank McPherson, David Myers, Carleton Paine, Natalie Porter, Clay Rivers, Martin Seligman, Rich Simon, and Brian Sugden.

To the late Charlie Gaston, Pat Kehoe, and Cliff Fawl. To Susan Lee Cohen, Jo Ann Miller, and Candace Taylor, and Ellen Garrison with respect and gratitude.

■ Introduction

In 1972 I saw my first therapy client, a young homeless woman from a brutal alcoholic family. Timidly and apologetically, Charlotte meandered into the free clinic at the university. Thereafter, in our weekly sessions, we struggled to make sense of her lonely, chaotic life. Charlotte would hang her head, her greasy bangs covering her eyes, as she whispered about rapes and beatings. She was so afraid of tenderness that, when I complimented her on even the smallest things, she winced. Six months into therapy, Charlotte pushed her hair away from her eyes and looked me in the face. By the end of our first year together, she would smile when we met and she even occasionally coughed out a tentative laugh. In the three years we worked together, I don't think I did her any harm. We liked and respected each other. No doubt I learned more from her than she learned from me.

Since then I have seen all kinds of people—hyperactive school boys, abused women, gifted students, gay dads, grieving widows, angry teenagers, adults who had committed various kinds of stupidity, psychopaths, people who were taking care of too many people, and families desperately trying to hold together or wrench apart. Over the last thirty years I've watched a lot of pain flow under the bridge.

By now I have a Ph.D. in human suffering. I have listened to many cautionary tales and seen the ways humans can hurt themselves and other people. I have learned vicariously what mistakes not to make. I have witnessed the train wrecks that follow extramarital affairs. I haven't had to gamble, use drugs, or keep secrets to realize that those behaviors are ultimately destructive. I have acquired a lifelong tuition-free education in the consequences of various choices.

During most of my years in clinical practice, I worked six blocks from home with my husband, Jim, and my good friend Jan. We created a "small is beautiful" office. Our kids cleaned it until they left home and then we cleaned it ourselves. We did our own billing and scheduled our own appointments. Once, a high-powered psychiatrist said to me, "I'll have my people call your people." I had to confess, "I have no people."

Over the decades the work changed a great deal. New theories marched to center stage, then exited quietly. We therapists frothed our way through the ditzy seventies and almost destroyed ourselves in the eighties, the era of recovered memory work. We traveled from endless, unstructured sessions to goal-focused short-term therapy. Family therapy, once our finest technique, has almost vanished. And yet, like Homer's "wine-dark sea," therapy is, "always changing, always the same."

I love the work. Sometimes people ask if it is depressing to spend all day listening to problems. I tell them, "I am not listening *to* problems. I am listening *for* solutions." Clients generally arrive when they want to make changes. They are paying for advice and are ready to listen. As a therapist, my experience is that unhappy clients become happier, that feuding couples start to enjoy each other, and that families settle down and work together. Not always, but usually, after a few sessions, I begin to hear stories of victories.

In therapy, as in life, point of view is everything. As a therapist, I am slightly detached from my clients' problems. I try to keep my eyes on the prize, which, while tailored for each client, is essentially the same. I want people to leave feeling calmer, kinder, and more optimistic. I want them to be more intentional in their choices and, in many cases, less impulsive in their appetites.

Robert Frost wrote, "Education elevates trouble to a higher plane." So does psychotherapy. It is a way of exploring pain and confusion to produce meaning and hope. This book consists of lessons I've learned from the people who have tromped into my office and flopped down on my old couch for conversations. It distills what I have learned from hundreds of hours of listening to people answer the question, "What brings you in today?"

Along with having sex, sleeping, and sharing food, conversation is arguably one of the most basic of all human behaviors. Two or more people tell each other stories. They struggle to solve the problems of their day and to laugh and calm down. Freud structured these conversations in a new way and academics eventually conducted research on these particular conversations but, in the end, therapy consists of people talking things over.

It is complicated work. Mark Twain described himself as "all of humanity crammed into a suit of clothes." Everyone who walks into our office contains all the rest of us. And yet, we all run from our humanity. We prevaricate and puff ourselves up. We fear admitting how vulnerable we feel. We try to hide our flaws. Over and over again, we have to learn how to simply be human.

In my case, I'm what a friend once described as a "clumsy brainiac." My mother joked I could write essays before I could walk. I am blind in one eye, moody, unfashionable, directionally impaired, claustrophobic, and easily tuckered out. And those flaws are just the ones I'll confess to. But somehow, I've found a few people to love me. And I know their flaws and love them, too. In fact, they are my close friends and family, the people I love the most.

As a therapist, I see myself as a generalist, the psychologist equivalent of my mother, who was a general practitioner of medicine. I am not a good play therapist. I treat young children by helping their parents figure out how to deal with them. I avoid legal work and sophisticated diagnostics. Specialization offers financial and professional rewards, but to me, specialization has always sounded dull. Thirty years is a long time to solve one kind of problem.

For me, the best trick is not to have tricks. When I attempt to be clever or sophisticated, I often confuse myself as well as my clients. Once when I suggested what I thought was a brilliant, rather mysterious, homework assignment, my client asked me if I was on drugs. Another time when I predicted the future in an attempt to generate a self-fulfilling prophecy, my hard-drinking client looked me in the eyes and said bluntly, "If you can predict the future, you ought to go to Vegas."

For the most part, my solutions to human problems have been simple ones—get more rest, do good work, take things a day at a time, and find some people to love. Of course, simple suggestions aren't necessarily easy and they don't always work. When they don't, I generally fall back on my belief in the process of therapy. Albert Einstein said, "A problem cannot be solved by the consciousness that created it." Therapy gives clients a safe relationship in which to explore their inner world and to consider taking risks in their external one. It provides them with another point of view on their own particular mixed-up universe.

As a student, I studied Carl Jung, Harry Sullivan, Otto Rank, Fritz Perls, and George Kelly. I read Freud, but I never much liked the idea that all good behavior was sublimation. I resisted his view that life was mostly competition, aggression, and sex—a very male theory. I was always attracted to growth and strength-based models. I respected the humanists and the existentialists— Abe Maslow, Rollo May, Victor Frankl, and Carl Rogers. I was intrigued by Carol Gilligan's and the Stone Center's ideas about the self in relationship to others. Even before Positive Psychology existed, I believed in the importance of focusing on good news.

When I began my training in 1972, psychologists were mainly testers. I learned to administer intelligence tests, personality inventories, and projectives, in which clients were shown indistinct stimuli, such as inkblots, and asked to report on what they saw. At first, I was fascinated by all those tests, but with experience I grew to prefer conversations as a diagnostic method.

I interned at the University of Texas Medical Center, which at that time had several pioneers of family therapy employed. I relished the liveliness of family therapy. Later at the University of Nebraska I taught one of the first Psychology of Women courses. In some ways I've swum in the mainstream, but I've also paddled alone. I had strong biases against family bashing, cutoffs, and blaming people who were not in the room to defend themselves. I urged clients to go home for holidays and attend family reunions. I never used the term "dysfunctional family" or recommended that anyone sue his own parents.

Even as a little girl, I felt protective of my own quirky family. I experienced my mother and father as rather incompetent, unavailable parents with many complicated problems of their own. But I also experienced them as loving me and doing their best. Much of my internal landscape comes from my conversations with them. I don't judge them harshly for their mistakes and I don't feel inclined to judge others too harshly either.

Perhaps because of my training in anthropology, I have always viewed mental health problems as related to the broader environment. Depression, anxiety, domestic violence, and drug and alcohol abuse, not to mention hyperactive children and eating disorders, arise from our deeply dysfunctional culture. Who can be healthy in a culture in which children watch movies about hookers and serial killers? How can we expect people to be happy when they don't know their neighbors, see their extended families, or have time for naps on Sunday afternoons?

As a culture, we are mired deep in denial about our effects on others, on the earth, and on generations to come. We ignore the problems of children, refugees, the aged, and the poor. Our media encourages us to live at a surface level, to think about window treatments instead of world peace or our own spiritual needs. We are educated to be compartmentalized. Our culture makes us sick, physically and emotionally.

Good therapy gently but firmly moves people out of denial and compartmentalization. It helps clients develop richer inner lives and greater self-knowledge. It teaches clients to live harmoniously with others. And it enhances existential consciousness and allows people to take responsibility for their effects on the world at large.

For me, happiness is about appreciating what one has. Practically speaking, this means lowering expectations about what is fair, possible, and likely. It means finding pleasure in the ordinary. I'm not a television-watcher or shopper and, as best I can, I steer people away from the idea that happiness is connected to having more, more, and more.

To be an adult means to accept the awesome responsibility of constantly making choices. I believe that after a certain age, with the exception of the chronically mentally ill and the profoundly mentally challenged, we are all responsible for our own lives. It's patronizing and contemptuous to believe otherwise. I encourage clients to understand and accept the past with all its complexity. Then I urge them to move on to create something beautiful for themselves and others. We all have our sorrows, but they don't exempt us from our duties.

I opened my private practice in 1979, and most of my practice took place during the golden age when therapists had plenty of time to help clients. Most people carried good insurance coverage for therapy and even factory workers could come in for extended periods and explore their issues at a leisurely pace. Therapists weren't expected to produce rapid concrete changes. When managed care slammed into our state, I ignored it. I had enjoyed too many years of doing things my own way. I couldn't tolerate outsiders calling the shots with my clients.

Recently I met a busy therapist who bragged his therapy was, "All killer, no filler." He claimed he could treat most people in four sessions. I could barely conceal my skepticism. Good therapy, like good cooking, takes time. Of course some clients and therapists abused the old system. But most of us used our time wisely. In the past, we could develop strong relationships with our clients. Now in the crunch to save time and money, therapists must work fast and demonstrate weekly progress. Much is lost in the process.

Over the years I worked for the University of Nebraska as a clinical supervisor for graduate students in psychology. Sometimes I drove to the university and sat in on sessions or watched my students work from behind a one-way mirror. Often the students carried their tapes of therapy to my home. We played them on my VCR and I offered tips and sympathy.

I have written this book in the form of letters to Laura, who was my favorite graduate student. Laura was in her twenties and single. She was open-minded, warm-hearted, and deeply in love with psychology. Like me, she was an outdoors person. Unlike me, she was a risk-taker who liked canoeing, roller blading, and rock climbing. Like most young therapists, Laura was a funny mix of scared and overconfident. She wanted to sample every kind of client, but she was easily overwhelmed.

I hope both therapists and general readers relish these letters. I offer plenty of clinical examples from my own work. I save quotations and I can't resist throwing in some of my favorites. I try to avoid popular psychology lingo and social science jargon, and yet I want to gently remind readers that in these harsh times, therapy can be a solution.

I wrote these letters in the early morning. My desk overlooks an old maple tree, my flower garden, and bird and squirrel feeding stations. The letters were a yearlong project and the seasons influenced my moods and my writing. (The reader may enjoy analyzing me for seasonal affective disorder!)

I began writing these letters on December 2, 2001, a bitterly cold day in Nebraska. We were just about to put to bed the year that included September 11. All of us were hopeful that the New Year might bring better tidings, but it was a dark time for the world. For me, these letters were a kind of vacation. They gave me an opportunity to focus on human-sized issues rather than global events.

Dear reader, I hope you find these letters both educational and fun. Indeed one of the things I have observed as a therapist is that fun is by no means trivial. It's one of the best things we have. So, settle yourself into a comfortable spot in the sunlight or by a fire. Make some peach tea and find a cat for your lap. Let's visit.

PART I: WINTER

1
■ Breadcrumbs

Dear Laura,

Last night I sorted through some old black-and-white photographs. In one of my baby pictures, I am asleep with a magazine on my chest. Even then, I "read" myself to sleep. In another, I pose joyfully in a high chair covered with dinner, happily stuffing cake into my mouth. Still today, good food is one of my greatest pleasures. Another photo shows me standing beside my brother Jake in front of a big, red brick building. It's our first day in a new school. We're dressed in ill-fitting, old-fashioned coats. We look skinny and scared, our eyes wide with alarm. He's leaning into me and I am holding his hand.

These pictures construct a breadcrumb trail through the forest of time that lies between the me who was born in the Ozark Mountains and the fifty five-year-old me who lives in Nebraska today. The girl who squeezed her brother's hand before marching into the schoolhouse echoes within the therapist who often says to clients, "Together we can make things better."

As an old man, Mark Twain said, "I have arrived at an age at which the things I remember most clearly never happened." Memory is constructed and reconstructed. It changes constantly and is as subjective as dreams. Still, I'd like to share my breadcrumb trail with you.

I lived first in a small house my dad built when he returned to Missouri after World War Two. A year later we moved to Denver so my mother could go to medical school. After she graduated, my family's trail meandered to a number of small Nebraska towns, and then to Kansas, where I graduated from high school in 1965. Four years later I received my undergraduate degree from the University of California at Berkeley. Afterward, I bummed around Europe and Mexico before I settled down to graduate school and, later, to life in Lincoln as a wife, mother, and psychologist. From the beginning, no matter where I have lived, I have been restless, talkative, and intense. I have liked people, the natural world, and books.

Certain defining moments shaped my thinking. I remember the night when I was three years old that I became a cultural relativist, although, of course, I didn't know the phrase at the time. This was in 1950, before antibiotics were widely used. My mother had lectured me frequently that, after my baths, I must immediately dry my feet and put on my socks so that I wouldn't catch cold. But one night my Aunt Agnes supervised me as I crawled out of her tiger-claw bathtub and toweled off my feet. She admonished me, "Good little girls dry their bottoms first and then put on their underpants." I was surprised that two women whom I deeply trusted could disagree on a subject of such vital importance.

My family life was an education in point of view. I was the oldest daughter in a big family with a doctor mother and a lab-technician father who, when he wasn't working in hospitals, took time to raise pigs, geese, and pigeons. My mother's people were Methodists from eastern Colorado, poor ranchers, but well-educated and civic-minded. My father's relatives were colorful, warm-hearted people from the Ozarks. I had a millionaire aunt who was liberal, a farmer uncle who voted for Barry Goldwater, and another uncle who sold wieners and lard and had no interest in politics at all. My Aunt Margaret's family spent a year traveling around the world. My grandmother Glessie May was married to a man who lived a long life and died without ever leaving Christian County, Missouri. He asked rhetorically, "Why would I want to leave paradise?" At our house, emotional people played cards with stoics. Sophisticates and provincials told long stories and Southern Baptists shared chicken dinners with Unitarians.

When we lived in Beaver City, Nebraska, members of our extended family would visit us for weeks at a time.

My cousins and I would roam the fields, hike down to Beaver Creek, or bike around town looking for action on the quiet streets. At night, the adults played cards and argued politics. When conversation flagged around midnight, my dad would bribe the others, "Would you stay up if I fried some T-bones and potatoes?"

I slept in a daybed just off the dining room and I stayed awake listening to the sound of grown-ups talking. As I listened, I asked myself: Why did certain people fall in love with each other? Why did one family forbid rock and roll and movies? Why did one uncle drink so much? Why did some relatives love FDR and others detest him? Why was one cousin a bully and another wonderfully patient with me?

I worked at my mom's office counting out pills and sterilizing rubber gloves and surgical equipment. I heard the nurses whisper about things that most kids didn't know—that the woman who cleaned the bank was a prostitute, that the rich farmer who sent my mother flowers wanted her to perform an abortion for his girlfriend, and that the laughing man who ushered us into church was dying of leukemia.

Every small town has a cast of characters right out of Shakespeare. I knew the town drunk, the saintly or bitter shut-ins, the old soldiers, and the gay choir director. My schoolteachers were of mixed caliber, some indifferent and ignorant, others fiercely dedicated to teaching us the chief exports of Peru and China and how to diagram sentences. I chatted with hardworking merchants, hoodlums with ducktail haircuts, a kind-hearted undertaker, and a hot-tempered mayor. Our next-door neighbors believed it was sinful to wear shorts in public. That meant his sons couldn't play basketball and none of the kids could swim at our public pool—a harsh religion indeed.

Another breadcrumb on the trail was my role as family leader. My parents were away from home most of the time and we kids experienced a great deal of benign neglect. Many times we trudged through a blizzard eight blocks to school only to discover that school was cancelled for the day. Summer mornings I would dish myself a bowl of ice cream for breakfast and then decide whether I'd rather spend the morning at the library or under our apricot tree playing with other kids. I was the planner and fixer in my family. Once when I was five, my aunt asked my dad if our family wanted to go on a picnic. He answered, "Ask Mary, she plans everything."

Some psychologists would immediately label me as a parental child, prematurely responsible, and they would tsk-tsk in sympathy. But I see it differently. I had an important family role, which offered me authority and autonomy. I learned very young the joys of working hard and being useful. I developed skills in cooking, caring for children, making decisions, and organizing people. I discovered that the way to get my needs met was to first meet the needs of others. If I could tell people stories, bake them cookies, and make them laugh, I would be loved.

The prejudice in my town was another breadcrumb. The crippled son of our drugstore owner once made the terrible mistake of trying to kiss another boy, and after that his life was a perpetual hell. To this day I shudder when I think of the punishment inflicted on him for being "different." There were twin brothers, Denny and Kenny, unwashed and neglected, who were teased mercilessly for the crime of being sons of a convicted murderer. Another kid, Herbert, had some kind of dental problem that caused him to spit and slobber when he spoke. Children wouldn't go near him because he had "germs." Finally there was Naomi Rainwater, a Native-American girl who attended our school. Students just totally ignored her, as if having brown skin made her invisible. Even as a kid, I sensed all this was wrong. I was too young to know what to do about it, but I didn't like it and I stayed out of cruel games. I wish I could say I stood up for the children I have mentioned but I didn't do that either. Maybe that is why I try to stand up for people now. I have something to atone for.

Our town was surrounded by prairie dog villages. A more remote place in America is hardly imaginable. The skies sparkled clearer then and I remember the Northern Lights and winter stars tense with frost. In the pre-television world, time unfurled slowly. I lazed under the elms in the town square visiting with old men and babies. I sipped limeade and read comics at the drugstore and at night, my friends and I sprawled in the grass, looked at the Milky Way, and told ghost stories.

I learned to depend on the natural world for comfort and entertainment. After rainstorms, I rescued baby birds and mice and once I raised a magpie to be my summer companion. In the spring, our family bought baby coyotes from bounty hunters and we played with them until fall. Then we released them by Beaver Creek. We picked up turtles and snakes off the highways and kept them in aquariums. I was outdoors every moment I could be and I learned that whenever I was bored or upset, Mother Nature would take care of me.

By the time I was twelve, I had read every children's book in our town library—not a great feat because the collection was small. I liked the biographies of Helen Keller, Albert Sweitzer, Eleanor Roosevelt, and Madame Curie. I loved *A Tree Grows in Brooklyn*, *The Good Earth*, and a book called *The Silver Sword* about heroic Polish children who survived without parents during World War Two.

At this age I also discovered the *Diary of Anne Frank* and it stunned me. For the first time, I encountered evil—not just misguided, impulsive, or confused actions, of which I had seen plenty, but truly evil ones. For weeks afterward, I didn't eat or sleep well. I couldn't imagine a point of view that allowed adults to murder children. My mind struggled to comprehend this new information about what humans could do to each other. But paradoxically, the story also taught me about heroism. Anne Frank remains my greatest hero.

Sometimes my books landed me in trouble. Once on a family vacation I was reading Erich Fromm's *The Art of Loving*. This was a popular psychology book exploring the nature of intimacy. My dad glanced with alarm at the title. He surmised I had descended into smutty material and threw my beloved book into our campfire.

Reading transported me all over the world; it entertained me and calmed me down when I was rattled from family arguments or a rough day at school. With books I could be in my family's kitchen stirring bean soup and also in London with David Copperfield, on the trail of jewel thieves with the Dana Sisters or Nancy Drew. My mind became roomier.

If we conceive of life as a calendar year, beginning with spring and ending in deepest winter, then I am in the late autumn of my life. This season encourages an examination of the past. The stuff I took for granted as a girl—long summer days when nothing happened, aunts canning tomatoes or making mincemeat pies, fall evenings smelling of burning leaves—makes me ache with longing as a middle-aged woman.

Laura, you are in the early summer of your life. I am curious to see how your seasons will unfurl. Next supervision session I'd like to hear more about your history. You told me that in school you were the student other kids talked to about their problems. Being a confidante is part of your breadcrumb trail, as it is for many in our field. An examination of your past can help you know yourself better. Knowing yourself helps with your life as well as with your work.

2
Virtues

December 26

Dear Laura,

I just returned from our family Christmas celebration. We gathered for a potluck dinner followed by plum pudding and a gift exchange. Over guacamole my niece told me she planned to be a webmaster, a profession not even invented when I was her age. We had a good talk about choosing a career, about the difference between being good at something and liking it, and about how work shouldn't be just about money. My niece told me she had heard there were jobs for webmasters in Tampa and she'd always wanted to live near a beach.

Our discussion led me to reflect on my own decision, made impulsively thirty years ago, to be a psychologist. Because I couldn't secure funding for graduate school in anthropology, I more or less bumbled into psychology.

On a whim, I walked into the campus psychological consultation center and met the director of the clinical program. He encouraged me to consider the Ph.D. program and guaranteed funding. I was damn lucky. I loved graduate school. I have been able to work as a therapist, consultant, teacher, writer, and speaker—all because I was a psychologist. Laura, I know you wonder if you have the talents to be a good therapist. Permit me to have an "Aunt Mary" conversation with you on that topic.

We therapists end up sitting in small, often uncomfortable rooms eight hours a day listening to one person after another talk about unresponsive mates, surly teenagers, and control-freak bosses. Unless we have abiding curiosity, hour after hour of such conversations can be tough slogging. We who like the work tend to be fascinated by the infinite variety of ways in which humans get themselves in and out of trouble.

Doing therapy requires energy, focus, and patience. It's not particularly remunerative or prestigious and, unless you are motivated by a desire to help others, you are unlikely to last. Therapist Harry Aponte said that he couldn't work with people unless he saw something of himself in them and they saw something of themselves in him. Just as respect tends to be mutual, so does contempt. Unless your basic feelings toward most people are positive, therapy is not for you.

One of my writing teachers once advised me, "If your message for the world is that life is shit, spare the reader." Not a bad dictum for therapists as well. People come into therapy when they feel whipped. A great deal of our work is about hope. I can still picture Kimberly, a beautiful pregnant woman with waist-length blond hair sobbing for fifty minutes, unable to talk after telling me, "I have MS." That first session I passed her Kleenex and listened. At the end I hugged her and invited her back in two days. During our second session we talked about her three young kids and her husband who wasn't much of a provider and who leaned on her for decision-making and emotional support. She cried some more. I said, "You have already done the hardest thing which is to face this problem." And I continued, "You'll get through this. You are stronger than you think. Your family will do their best." At the end of that second session I asked, "What can you do to cope with the next few days?" Tearfully Kimberly answered, "Tonight I'll take my girls to the park."

Hope was my primary gift to Svetlana, a shy girl who was the victim of much teasing in middle school. By the end of the ninth grade, she had internalized all her peers' scorn and no longer believed in herself. As I got to know her I discovered her love of animals and her wry sense of humor. I helped her find a place she could ride horses and supported her decision to take a volunteer job at the Humane Society. Svetlana developed new skills, which built up her confidence. Her work with animals carried her away from her mean-spirited classmates to older, wiser people.

I made a few predictions. "Over the summer you will be surprised by moments of happiness and confidence.

Next year, you will meet a kindred spirit." For the most part my predictions came true. The summer of horses was a happy one and in the fall Svetlana marched bravely into high school. She did make a good friend, but she told me, "I'd rather shovel manure than face the 100 percent screwed-up-ness that is high school." Fair enough, I conceded. I couldn't fix everything.

Most of us are in this work for deeply personal reasons that we need to acknowledge. I grew up nurturing and caretaking as the "big sister." But alas, I'm also pretty good at being bossy and overly responsible. I have to watch both of these tendencies as a therapist.

We need to recognize when we are getting our clients mixed up with our mother, our elementary school principal, or our first boyfriend. We need to know whom we can help and whom we can't. For example, I am lousy at working with violent men. They scare me and I can't forgive them for hurting women and children.

While I don't think we therapists need to be paragons of mental health, I do think we need to be reasonably well-adjusted. Addicts, psychopaths, and self-deluded therapists damage vulnerable clients. We need good people skills. I acquired mine as a waitress. All through high school, I was a carhop at an A & W Root Beer stand. In college, at various greasy spoons and donut shops, I dealt with crabby, persnickety customers, and with snobs, drunks, and cheapskates. I also met charmers, jokers, and some of the kindest folks imaginable. By the time I figured out how to get along with John Q

Public, I had a good education in the vagaries of humanity.

Graduate students whom the other students avoid because they are abrasive or strange had best seek other work. My class included one "psychonoxious" therapist. Rob was a bitter, sarcastic person who seemed to enjoy making other people feel small. As our introductory therapy class watched Rob's sessions on videotape, we squirmed in our seats. When he tested a patient at our state mental hospital, he precipitated a psychotic break in his client. When he saw his first client, a depressed English major, he soon had her in tears with his hostile questions. ("Do you really expect me to believe that? Are you trying to manipulate me? Why didn't you do something more intelligent?") Our teacher looked stunned and remained silent. But a few weeks later, Rob transferred into experimental psychology where he worked mostly with rats.

One of the luxuries of our work is that it sustains idealism. Unlike cops, landlords, or bar owners, therapists tend to grow fonder of humans the longer they are in our field. That's because we come to understand the world from the point of view of others. We see that most people want to be good.

Being a client was one of my best lessons in being a therapist. When I first called for an appointment, my voice cracked with embarrassment. I felt stupid and vulnerable. I learned how hard it was to admit failures and to share secrets with a stranger. I cared desperately about what my therapist thought and I took his smallest remarks seriously. I noticed what kind of pens he used and when he blinked.

My therapist was a low-key guy without pretensions. I saw him at his house Saturday mornings. His wife would hand me a cup of coffee and show me to his small office. He would smile, ask me what was up, and then really listen to what I had to say. He didn't analyze me and rarely gave advice. Sometimes he made small jokes. Mainly he was kind.

Once when I was trying to describe how I felt, he gently suggested the word "angry." At precisely the moment I was ready to do so, he helped me identify a feeling I couldn't easily acknowledge.

Good therapists have a tolerance for ambiguity. The human condition is variegated, multifaceted, and particular. There is no one-size-fits-all way to proceed. In the end, the answer to most questions is, "It depends." Rigid therapists who think, it's my way or the highway, are flops. Their black-and-white smugness drives clients, who live in gray worlds, crazy. In our town, there's a therapist who is a one-trick pony. All his clients, no matter what their problems or personalities, receive his brand of confrontive, behavioral-focused, short-term therapy, which can be useless or even harmful to some clients.

Labeling a problem as "complex" is one of my more effective therapeutic approaches. Clients appreciate not being pigeonholed. It is a way of respecting people to describe their situations as complicated. If problems felt simple, clients wouldn't be in therapy. Complex is a nonjudgmental word that buys time and space. It suggests that circumstances may be examined for new and surprising revelations.

Therapists need to be able to sort true from untrue, deep from shallow, and temporary from long-term. We need what Hemingway referred to as "foolproof shit detectors." Muddled thinking and mealy mouthed affirmations never help anyone. I once met a sweet but fuzzy-headed therapist at a psychotherapy institute. She told me that she gave unconditional positive regard to everyone, even psychopaths and borderlines. She quoted the Beatles: "All you need is love." I thought to myself, "clients need much more than that. Almost all need clarity and perspective and a few need a figurative kick in the butt."

Nonjudgmental can mean indiscriminate and openness can mean rudderless. Our field has its share of space cadets, strange agents, and woo-woo practitioners. Good therapists walk a balance beam between maintaining old-fashioned common sense and encouraging new ideas. We can never know for sure that our understanding is profound or our advice apropos. Much of our work is not hard science. Rather, therapy includes science, intuition, and kindness. What really works in therapy is a real person connecting to a real person.

Don't be intimidated by what may look like a formidable list of virtues. These qualities occur naturally in most of the people interested in our field. That's why we work as therapists; we thrive on tackling human problems. Laura, except for years of experience, you possess everything you need to be a great therapist.

3

■ M o t h e r   N a t u r e   D e l i v e r s

January 3

Dear Laura,

We are in what the Lakota called the moon of popping trees, so named because this time of year ice storms break tree branches with a loud pop. Next month will be the moon of frost in the tepees. Late March brings the moon of snow blindness. These names for moons give us a glimpse into the Lakota's connection to their environment. I wish we used these names today.

I am putting away my holiday decorations and looking one last time at Christmas cards. My client Sandra sent me a picture of her dog. This year Placido stands in a garden with his tongue out and an American flag around his neck. Sandra makes her living frying donuts. She has built her life around Placido, who gives her what she has of contentment and friendship. Over the years I have received a drawer full of Placido pictures. They remind me how important pets can be for people.

Many clients have been rescued by their relationships to animals. Donella always wanted a pet, but had a long list of reasons she shouldn't have one. She was allergic to cat hair, had a studio apartment, and couldn't afford cat food, kitty litter, and vet bills. But after September 11, Donella couldn't concentrate at work. She went to the Humane Society and selected a Siamese kitten. She said, "Without Sofie I'd be on Prozac and Metamucil."

Losing pets is a much more painful experience than most people anticipate or than our culture generally acknowledges. Many clients apologize as they sob over the loss of a pet. They say, "I feel stupid being so upset about this." But often they add, "I am crying more about this loss than I cried when my parents died." Pets work their way deep into our hearts, but in our human-centric culture we can't afford to admit this.

In a Jane Goodall film called *Children and Nature*, kids with serious psychological problems were sent to a camp where they were allowed to choose pets for themselves. At first, the staff watched the kids closely to make sure they would not abuse the animals. Sadly, hurting animals is common in disturbed children. Gradually, the children grew fond of the animals and selected their own pets. Then many of the children hesitated to touch their pets for fear they would hurt them. These kids had never experienced themselves as anything but destructive, and now they expected that they would accidentally destroy what they loved. As they cared for their animals and developed relationships with them, they realized that their pets were dependent on them in order to survive, and the children experienced their first unconditional positive regard.

Animals don't live in clock-time, let alone computer-time or microwave-time. Recently, I walked at the state fair among the kids displaying their cattle. I thought to myself, these cattle are moving at exactly the same speed today as cattle moved a thousand years ago. In 2003, it's therapeutic for kids to slow down to the speed of cattle.

Rhythms synchronize. "Entrainment" refers to a biological law that states when organisms are together they soon match rhythms. When we are in the natural world we slow down. Then, amazing things happen. Last August my daughter-in-law and I lay down on a blanket and watched the Perseid meteor showers. As we breathed the cool grassy air and counted the stars falling, we had one of the finest conversations in our relationship. We talked about life in outer space, death, God, and time.

Laura, you know about the effects of nature from your rock climbing and canoeing. As you move at the speed of a river, your breathing changes. Your senses open up to the smell of trees and the sounds of splashing water. The Xhosa people of South Africa believe that a human community will be cursed and die when no one notices the rising and setting of the sun and the phases of the moon. I am inclined to agree. If we are too out of touch to notice the "moon when the cherries turn black," what is it we are in touch with?

Perhaps the greatest gift we receive from the natural world is the moment when we understand something that is deeply important. Theoretically we can have epiphanies in shopping malls, but that is not where they generally come to us. Epiphanies burst forth when it's quiet and slow.

Jim and I once camped with folksinger Butch Hancock. We journeyed through Big Bend National Park on the Texas/Mexican border. In the park, ocutillo flowers blossomed like flames on the ends of their long candle branches. Javelinas and coyotes foraged in tamarisk, belladonna, and mesquite. We canoed up the Rio Grande most of the day. Early evening, we pitched our tents and talked while we cooked dinner. Even though I was on the river, my conversation was political and my mood gloomy, reflecting the cloudy sky and the weary chill we all must have been feeling. Just then, the sun broke out and flamed the canyon walls an iridescent bronze. Butch turned to me and said, "Look. Look. This is the kind of thing that really can happen." I am not sure Butch meant this remark as profoundly as I heard it. For me it was a metaphor. When I am discouraged, I remember that blazing canyon wall and tell myself, "Look at the good things that can happen."

Laura, you can't orchestrate epiphanies, but you can suggest walks at sunset and blankets on the grass on starry nights. Then you can cross your fingers and hope that a goose flies across the face of the moon or that catalpa flowers blow down on your clients like snow.

Whenever you are working with people who live in their heads, consider recommending a pet. There is nothing like a kitten playing in front of a fire to calm you down. After a long day at the office, most humans can benefit from the manic warmth of a loyal dog's greeting. Next time you're in my office, I'll show you my most recent picture of Placido.

4
▪ Family Bashing

Dear Laura,

Annie Dillard writes that, "A day spent reading is a day well spent," an observation most befitting February. This time of year I spend most evenings by my fire reading. Usually I start with work-related books and articles, but after an hour or so I switch to an old favorite like Cather or Trollope. Outside it's a deep freeze, black except for the brittle stars, but inside it's bright and warm. The contrast feels delicious.

Last night I read a case history about deep brief therapy, an approach that lasts a few sessions but profoundly changes the clients involved. It struck me as a bogus concept. Relationships take time. When we suggest that high-quality advice can be given under rushed conditions, we undercut what we can offer people—a calm place to carefully explore their situations. Further-more, we are likely to harm people if, while we are igno-rant about many aspects of their lives, we jump in with radical advice and grandiose plans to transform them.

The case history concerned an African-American woman who was living with a man she didn't particu-larly like and working at a job she hated. She had been on antidepressants and described herself as chronically miserable. The therapist asked about her family and she recalled a hurtful comment her mother had made to her at a funeral. He seized on that remark as the cause of his client's depression. He felt the mother had permanently stifled his client's ability to express her feelings. He ignored other possible problems, such as his client's bad job, unresponsive partner, and lack of friends. For that matter, he didn't look into her exercise habits, alcohol and drug use, or the significant prob-lems facing black women in this country. Instead, he helped his client get in touch with her rage against her mother. Based on the one remark from his client, the therapist demonized her mother in order to manufac-ture a brief, deep experience. What's wrong with this picture? With almost no information, this therapist en-couraged his client to rewrite her history and replan her future. Parenthetically, he discussed the impor-tance of honoring subjective truth, a fuzzy phrase that describes what clients feel happened in the past. That concept seems to me a prescription for trouble. The therapist built a skyscraper on a meringue.

Many clients come to us because their subjective truths are twisted in ways that distort their lives. One of our most important jobs is to help clients examine these subjective truths and replace them with a more authentic reality.

I don't know what the mother in the case history was like, but neither did the client's therapist. All children have grievances. No one really feels understood. I love Shep Walker's line in *Divine Secrets of the Ya-Ya Sisterhood*. When he was asked, "Did you get enough love?" he answered, "What's enough?"

The therapist made the shaky assumption that if the daughter was unhappy, it must be the family's fault. In fact, the relationship between parenting and successful children is complex and unpredictable. Honest parents don't always raise honest kids. One of the most wholesome women I know grew up with an alcoholic mother. Some of the unhappiest adults I've met come from sensitive, child-focused families. Well-meaning couples sometimes have extraordinarily bad luck with their kids, while slapdash parents may raise highly successful children. In fact, in one family the siblings can cover the mental health gamut.

Ever since Freud, psychologists have seen families as hotbeds of pathology. We have taught therapists to ferret out the sick dynamics, hidden messages, and unrealistic pressures that families inflict on their members. We have encouraged clients to recall slights, mistakes, and times they were hurt or misunderstood. During the recovered memory era, we even "helped" clients remember traumas they had forgotten.

After thirty years as a therapist I know terrible things happen in families. I once saw a hairdresser mother who got angry with her daughter and scalded her head. I have counseled incest victims and children abandoned by their parents. I watched middle-aged businessmen cry when they talked of their relationships with mean-spirited fathers. But I also believe that we can't hate our families without hating ourselves.

Historically therapists have used the dysfunctional family as an explanation for adult misery and failure. In doing this we have largely ignored the effects of culture—of meaningless jobs, long commutes, sterile suburbs, and fears of poverty, war, violent death, and environmental catastrophes. And we have overlooked what people have known since time began: Life makes most of us unhappy.

Many of our psychological theories are not family friendly. We have used positive words such as "autonomy" and "independence" to praise distance and negative words such as "codependent" and "enmeshed" to punish closeness. With terms like "emotional incest," we have framed many loving acts as pathological and we have utterly confused people about the nature of love. We have elaborated on what families do to people but we haven't articulated what families do *for* people. We have encouraged clients to pursue their own dreams without considering an aging grandmother who craves a visit, children who yearn for attention, or a sibling who needs an ally.

While families are imperfect institutions, they are also our greatest source of meaning, connection, and joy. I remember a mother in her early forties whose three kids were in high school and about to fly the coop. She was in therapy to deal with anticipatory grief. She said, "I wish I could build a moat around our acreage and just keep us all together. We have had such great times." I recall our daughter at five, nuzzling into her father and saying, "I'm melting into richness."

Of course, as therapists we discuss hurt and angry feelings. And sometimes clients need to set limits and make position statements about what they will and won't tolerate in their families. But our goal should always be to strengthen families. Even for clients from the most abusive families we can say, "Find someone to love that is family. Even if it is your second cousin twice removed, seek out that person and build a family relationship. Everyone needs kin."

Families come to us when they are stuck. Often that means that the way the family is trying to solve at least one problem is making things worse. A wife wants her husband's attention so she complains. He feels bullied and withdraws even further. Or parents want a teenager to talk to them so they pester her for information and she responds by becoming more secretive, so they pester her more.

As I write about stuck families, I think of the Wilsons. The dad was a leather-clad biker with curly red hair. His two sons wore the same black leather jackets and had the same flowing red curls. The family was in therapy because, just like their father before them, the boys were flunking out of high school. The parents insisted the boys study, but the sons demonstrated their manhood and their identification with their father by resisting school and homework. When they were in my office the Wilsons spoke gravely of grades and teachers' conferences. But when I ran into them one afternoon at a Dairy Queen, they were laughing over banana splits. Then they put on their helmets and roared off into the sunset. Seeing the Wilson family out in the real world reminded me that therapy is only a small part of our clients' lives. We have a responsibility not to screw up the other parts that work.

Since I was in graduate school, our field may have slightly softened its harsh views of families. We've had a positive psychology movement and many clinicians have re-thought their attitudes. As the culture grows more toxic, most therapists are aware of the difficulties that parents face. We see that many families need to be supported rather than analyzed. Still, Laura, you will experience plenty of family bashing in supervision sessions, books, and classrooms. I urge you to take it all with a full shaker of salt.

All families are a little crazy, but that is because all humans are a little crazy. When we alienate clients from their families we assume an enormous responsibility. If we take away belief in family, what do we replace it with? If people don't trust their families, who is it they can trust?

When a client tells you that you are much more understanding than his wife, you can say, "But I don't see you every morning at the breakfast table. It's easier for me to be detached. I only have to deal with you one hour a week and I don't have to convince you to mow the yard." When a client begins, "I grew up in a dysfunctional family," you can say, "Let's not worry too much about what we call your family. What actually happened?" When a client moans, "My parents are responsible for my despair," you can say, "We can talk about that, but we can also talk about what you can do to be happier."

Families for all their flaws are one of our remaining ancient and true shelters. Families, not therapists, will be there for our clients if they lose their jobs, go to the hospital, or need someone to show up at their bowling tournaments. To quote poet Robert Frost, "Home is where when you have to go there they have to take you in." He also wrote in the same poem, families are "something you somehow haven't to deserve."

When you see families, don't forget that they have solved a thousand problems without your help. You will be seeing them in the February of their lives, but it won't always be February. June will come. Tread lightly. Do not fix what is not broken.

5
■ Deepening Therapy

February 7

Dear Laura,

I was stranded for the last few days at my grand-daughter's home in Iowa. As we snuggled inside, watching road reports on television and the blizzard outside, I never felt happier. Kate is an eight-month-old feast for the senses. She is fun to touch, look at, and listen to as she coos her various adorable sounds. I enjoy watching my son dance with Kate much like my father danced with me. Only Zeke and Kate dance to Van Morrison, while my father and I danced to Duke Ellington.

In my granddaughter's eyes, I see the eyes of my grandmother Glessie. In some of her gestures, I envision my mother. After these visits, I think about time passing and about how, if I am lucky, I will know seven generations of my family—from my Great-Granny Lee to

Kate's children. I think about the role I can play in her life. I want Kate to become all she can be so that she can use her gifts in the service of humankind.

Psychologist Frank Pittman calls this lifelong process of development, "growing a soul." Clients usually come to us with a specific problem. They come when they've been arrested for shoplifting, can't sleep, or feel anxious about a crappy job they are afraid to quit. They suffer from an eating disorder, or have a relationship derailing, or child who is failing in school. Generally they want to alleviate their crises quickly and with minimal effort. Sometimes we can help them do that. Other times, these presenting problems are connected to everything else. Specific problems turn out to be metaphors or symptoms of much larger issues.

A mother showed up at my office with her son, who had been arrested for hacking into the school's computer system. This boy often stayed up at night playing computer games. He had a secret life, not only with computers, but also with friends, money, and time. The mother divorced years ago and the boy no longer knew his father. They lived far from extended family. Formulating solutions involved truly understanding this mom, her son, and the environment they functioned in.

Another woman dressed in tight blue jeans, high heels, and a low-cut sweater, complained that her husband no longer spent time with her. She suspected he was having an affair. She said, "I work out at the gym every day and weigh exactly what I weighed when we got married." She added, "If he is having an affair, I am going to kill myself." I asked her, "What else do you have in your life besides your husband?"

Deepening therapy involves taking surface complaints and connecting them to deeper issues. Sometimes it requires confrontive questions such as, "Do you feel you have been a good father?" Other times it involves soothing questions such as, "Isn't it time to forgive yourself for this?" More philosophical clients eventually arrive at Paul Gauguin's famous questions: "Where do we come from? Who are we? Where are we going?"

Most children receive feedback about their behavior, but generally adults are on their own. No one tells them, "You talk with your mouth full," "Sit up straight," "You need to comb your hair and put on a different shirt," or "Stop sulking when you don't get your way." Clients think, feel, and behave in therapy in the same ways they do in real life. We can be of great service to them if we can figure out what they most need to hear and then tell them in a way that allows them to listen.

That doesn't always happen. I worked with a CEO who considered people interesting objects designed to serve and entertain him. Donald came in because he had a hard time keeping women in his life. He had an easy time attracting them and even getting them to bed. But as he put it, "The only ones who stick around have cash registers for hearts." Once after a therapy session, which at that time cost $45, Donald handed me a hundred dollar bill and said, "Keep the change." I shoved his money back and asked, "What are you trying to do to this relationship?"

I posed questions to him: "Who are the people you truly love and respect? Are there any people who care about you? How will your life be remembered by others? What difference will you have made to the earth?"

But I bombed with Donald. He had a value system in which relationships were secondary to making money. He respected Donald Trump and Bill Gates, but regarded his parents and adult siblings as nuisances he had to see once or twice a year on holidays. There weren't many people in his world who would remember him fondly. I did feel a bit of hope when I asked him about what difference his life would make. He looked at me almost sadly and said, "None of us matters in the end. We're all worm's meat." That was an answer we could have discussed had he stayed in therapy. But I couldn't meet his needs quickly enough and he left. In the end, I was just one more service worker who let him down.

As a beginning therapist, I was trained to ask many variants of the question, "How did others treat you and how do you feel about that?" Over the years my job has evolved into helping people think about the effects of their behaviors on others. Now I am more likely to ask, "How did you treat others and how did you make them feel?"

Good therapy should rearrange the landscape of the mind. After therapy, people live in the world differently. Behavior may change. A client who always associated anger with violence may learn that anger can be discussed. Often people think and feel differently. The wife accepts that her husband's way of showing love is by running errands. The daughter realizes her father can never be who she wants him to be, but that she can enjoy him anyway.

It's all about balance. I encourage anxious, timid people to become stronger and bolder. I try to help macho men be gentler and more expressive. I remember Ken, a man who could never outrun his appetites for alcohol, gambling, and women. I encouraged him to slow down. I asked him, "What could you ask yourself before you drink, or gamble, or have sex with a stranger?" I encouraged Ken to spend a few minutes a day sitting alone with no distractions, breathing slowly, and noticing his feelings. Ken deeply feared slowing down, and when he finally did, he was depressed by the wasteland that was his internal life. After a few weeks of experiencing sad feelings, he began to make slightly better decisions.

Many rigid thinkers see only extremes as possible solutions to problems. I push them to consider other options. I ask, "Are there aspects of this problem you are overlooking? I wonder if others might see this differently?" Once I saw an old man whose son never came to visit him. He could only imagine two choices for himself: disowning his son or giving all his money to the boy after his death. I asked him, "Could you bequeath him part of your estate? Could you perhaps tell your son that you are lonely?"

I ask busy people to slow down and people with stag-
nating lives to get something cooking. I try to energize
slugs and calm down clients who are addicted to their
own adrenaline. Sad people sometimes need help ex-
pressing anger. I say, "Start ten sentences in a row with
the opening words, 'I am angry about. . . .'" Conversely,
I encourage angry people to experience the deep sadness
that lies under anger. I ask, "What feeling hurts even
more than anger?" I suggest impulsive people think
carefully and I encourage ruminators to take action. I try
to help selfish people be more thoughtful and self-sacri-
ficing people to take better care of themselves. Together
clients and I search for the golden mean.

Years ago I made a speech in Japan. I was impressed
that in the Japanese language there are many words that
describe having two or even three feelings at once. English has only a few such words, "bittersweet," maybe
"poignant." But in fact, most of the time we are feeling
more than one thing. When I leave a family reunion, I
am relieved to be in my quiet car and sad to be saying
goodbye. When I am angry with my husband, I am also
sympathetic that he may be doing his best. Watching a
sunset, my heart can break two ways at the same time:
joy at its beauty and sorrow at the shortness of life. Even
though English doesn't have beautiful Japanese feeling
words, we can help clients describe the skeins of feelings
that make up complex emotional states. We can ask,
"What other feelings are you having right now?" When
we do, we take things to another level.

Elizabeth Barrett Browning wrote, "The earth is crammed with heaven." The older I get, the more I value life in all its manifestations, the more precious it seems to be granted the gift of time on our great blue and green planet. The biggest tragedy for me is when something beautiful wants to grow and something else stops it.

I want my granddaughter, Kate, to blossom into a human who loves the world and works to save it. And I want that for all my clients. It's easier to see potential in my cooing, dancing granddaughter, but it is there in the CEO who tried to leave a tip and in the entitled teenager who complained about her parents. Laura, in all of us, the potential to be good is there, if only someone will take the time to help us discover it and make it bloom.

6
■ Connecting the Dots

February 28

Dear Laura,

I can describe my mother's hands perfectly. They were tanned, with freckles, liver spots, and wormy blue veins snaking across their backs. The fingernails were clean, unpainted, and cut short. Her translucent skin, as thin as paper, slipped over the delicate bones on the backs of her hands. I can describe her hands so precisely because my mother's hands are my hands now.

Time moves on. In families and professions, one generation replaces another. Many of our great therapists have retired or died. At one time, there were many therapists who flew by the seat of their own charisma. Fritz Perls, Carl Whitaker, Sal Minuchin, and Virginia Satir come to mind. Milton Erickson, the greatest of all gurus, had a way of cutting through Gordian knots by making droll observations. Once he transformed a troubled therapist who had come to him for supervision by giving him a posthypnotic suggestion to climb a mountain.

As a young therapist, I was seduced by wizardry, but I gradually realized that elaborate strategies, duplicitous techniques, and complicated paradoxes are not my strong suits. I'm not sexy or edgy. Straightforward methods are less likely to bewilder me or my clients. Plus, they feel more respectful. I try to treat clients the way I would want to be treated. Only if these methods fail do I turn to more sophisticated techniques.

I do bread-and-butter work. I celebrate victories and record happy events as well as troubles. I almost always give homework assignments. My generic assignments are—have some fun, do a good deed, and get some exercise. I save the last few minutes of each session to discuss our hour together. I ask, "How do you feel about how we worked together today?" "Did we make a dent in your problems?"

I disconnect my phone during sessions and I don't allow cell phones or pagers. When clients arrive rushed and stressed, I suggest we sit quietly and breathe deeply for a few moments before we talk. Likewise, when people are sobbing, I've learned to wait. Therapy isn't radio. We don't need to constantly fill the air with sounds. Sometimes, when it's quiet, surprising things happen. A woman will sigh and admit she no longer loves her husband. A man will whisper, "I never told anyone this. . ." and begin to cry.

Inspiration is very polite. She knocks softly and then goes away if we don't answer the door.

Outside America is noisy. In an era of nanoseconds and sound bites, therapists work in real time. To quote my friend Vicki Robin, "We slow people down to the speed of wisdom." With our tone, words, facial expressions, and body posture, we convey, "We're in this together. Whatever happens we can handle it."

Persistence is an underrated virtue in our profession. Some of therapy is just plain plodding. Looking at the eating journals of bulimic women, talking to a depressed college student about exercise, or checking with a mother on her use of time-outs—these things don't feel like making magic or yield impressive workshop videos. But, like brushing teeth and eating fresh vegetables, they matter.

Change that looks too good to be true most likely is. Just as there is no free lunch, there is no free transformation. I favor incremental change. My model for this is Dr. Suzuki, who developed a method for teaching children to play classical music. He discovered that if steps are small enough anyone could move forward into mastery. People rarely try to take giant steps, and if they do they often fall down. The trick is finding the step size that propels people forward but allows them to succeed with each move.

A person who is always turning a corner often finds himself driving around the same block. I encourage clients, "Don't rush and don't stop." I praise what I hope will continue. I might say to a troubled teenager, "I really like it that you went to school when you felt tired. That shows real maturity."

I inquire, "What has worked before?" One of my chronically mentally ill clients told me of going to a new psychiatrist. The doctor had a two-feet-tall pile of her treatment records on his desk. But he didn't open the charts. Instead he asked my client, "Have you ever had any medications that worked?" My client answered, "As a matter of fact I have," and told him exactly the mix of drugs. The doctor wrote her a prescription for them and she began to improve immediately.

I embed positive thoughts and suggestions into questions—"How can you use your strengths to solve this problem? How will you know when you have truly made some progress? How many times a day do you laugh? How would a close friend improve your situation? What would change if you stopped letting the kids run your life?"

I often ask clients to bring in pictures of their families and significant others. Usually people look different than I had pictured them or than my client had described them. The evil father looks like a sick old man. The dominating mother looks self-deprecating and eager to please. The handsome boyfriend looks slovenly, homely, and totally resistible. Photos often give clients a memory jolt and they share fresh observations and new stories. Usually both the client and I feel more accountable to the family after we look at pictures. On the other hand, many times clients show me pictures of themselves smiling and then say, "I was actually miserable in that picture." Then they'll tell behind-the-scenes stories. I'm convinced that a lot of posing goes on, literally and figuratively, during picture taking.

Sometimes clients must be challenged. I've had to say, "I can't allow you to drive a school bus while you are smoking pot." Or, "Your wife is doing all the work in your family. Do you think that is fair?" With challenges, tone is everything. With a gentle caring tone, we can be confrontive and still maintain warm relationships with our clients.

Reframing can inspire change. If a mother and daughter fight all the time, I might say, "It looks like you both work constantly to stay connected to each other." About a stubborn child, I can remark, "This perseverance will serve him later in life if properly applied." To a man who complains that his wife always messes up the morning paper, I can say, "Every day she gives you a lovely reminder that you are not alone."

I have learned to attend my own feelings. If I noticed I was stifling yawns with a client, I would ask myself, "Is the client talking without thinking, or repeating old statements we've both heard before?" Once I stopped a session in which my client was talking fast and nonstop about superfluities. I said, "I have the feeling all this chatter is a diversion of some type. What's going on?"

My client fell silent and, for a moment, she looked as if I had shot her. Then she said softly and for the first time, "I want out of my marriage."

Laura, pay attention to your own feelings and use them in the session. The reactions you have to your clients are most likely the same ones that others have. If someone always irritates you with no-shows, lateness, or forgotten checks and assignments, that's information about why they have trouble in relationships.

We can help clients look through the triple lens of time—the past, present, and future. The past informs every moment of our lives. As we say to young women with eating disorders, "Nobody eats alone." We can ask, "Does the way your dad handled stress remind you of yourself with your daughter?" Or, "How is the choice you are making today going to affect your future?"

Humans do three things—we think, feel, and behave. Often humans are compartmentalized and don't connect the dots between these activities. This compartmentalization can be dangerous. People can feel angry and discouraged and not connect that feeling with their heavy drinking and television watching.

Our best work helps clients make connections. "Do you think your depression is related to your cutting benefits to the workers at your factory?" Or, "Are you aware that you think a great deal about your son but you actually spend very little time with him?" And, "Did you notice that whenever your wife leaves town you play poker?" Or,

"Have you observed that when you talk about your daughter, you hold your arms over your heart?"

If the secret of successful real estate is location, location, location, the secret of our work is connection, connection, connection. We need to connect affect, behavior, and thinking. We want our clients connected to us, their families, and to other people. I recall Miriam, a highly sensitive client, awash in feelings and housebound from anxiety. She loved to process her emotions, but she needed to do something different. I encouraged her to take small but courageous actions. She could walk to the grocery store a couple of blocks from her house. She could call her friends on the phone. And she needed to think, not emote her way through life. I recommended she write out her feelings and the irrational thoughts that triggered them. Then she could write out more rational thoughts that would perhaps allow her to feel better. I encouraged her to sign up for yoga.

You can unstick sessions by being aware of this ABC triangle of affect, behavior, and cognition. Whenever anyone is talking too much in one dimension, ask about the other two dimensions. Another way to help is to connect clients' present with the past or future.

In tragic situations, talking about good times can be therapeutic. When my mother was dying, she spent many months in a hospital, in pain, vomiting, and often unable to sleep. Toward the end, when I often stayed the night with her, we happened upon a game. We pretended she wasn't in a hospital. We were on a camping trip, like many we had taken to the Rocky Mountains. I told her to smell the pine trees and breathe the cool mountain air. The bubbling of her oxygen machine was a waterfall, the bed a sleeping bag, and the ceiling sparkled with constellations. She smiled and drifted off counting stars.

My generation's wave will be the next to break on the shore. Soon, Laura, you'll be doing the work I do now. I hope this advice helps you enrich the lives of those you see.

■ PART II: SPRING

7
■ Pain

March 23

Dear Laura,

Jim and I just returned from our annual trip to see the migrating sandhill cranes. It was a cold, drizzly trip. Except for the occasional blaze of forsythia, Nebraska was dressed in earth tones—oyster, brown, tan, and gray. Most people would complain about that weather, but I hold that there is no bad weather, just bad clothes. I enjoy the earth in all her costumes.

By yesterday there were a half million cranes roosting on the Platte River. As a species, they are almost as old as the Rocky Mountains. They flew over Nebraska when it was an inland sea. During the day the cranes dance in the cornfields; at sunset, thousands wheel onto the Platte forming their own dark islands in the quiet river. They trill a call, which naturalist Paul Gruchow described as "the sound of something you heard before you were born." I find comfort in observing their ancient rituals. They put my little life in perspective. Instead of making me feel insignificant, they make me feel like a small part of something infinite.

Right now you are working with several traumatized clients and I encourage you to go see the cranes as a way to relax.

Years ago I worked with a client named Lorena. She was a social worker who loved to sing and dance to folk music. A single mother, she lived with her three kids in one of our poorest neighborhoods. I saw her during what she called "the year of the locusts." Her youngest daughter had a seizure at school and was diagnosed with epilepsy. She lost her closest friend to breast cancer and her dad died of a heart attack while trying to catch the bus. The first time I saw her all she could do was cry. Then at the end of our session she dried her tears, thanked me, and said, "I thought I wanted to come. I needed to come."

For a time, sorrow overwhelmed Lorena. As she put it, she "trudged through a gray tapioca fog." But she was a strong woman and she gradually learned to accept all her feelings rather than run from them.

Many people have years of tough times. I remember talking to a young Kurdish refugee about her work. Her back and shoulders ached from long days in a cold, slippery locker at a meat packing plant. I said something about this not being an easy time for her. Jabha replied, "Never in my life have I had one day that was easy."

In *Another Country*, I wrote about Alma, aged eighty-two, widowed, going deaf, and almost blind from diabetes. She lived with her profoundly retarded, sixty-year-old daughter in a small house. But Alma cheerfully did what needed to be done. She made friends with her postman, neighbors, and visiting nurses. She played practical jokes on her family and even on me when I stopped by. (It was actually the first time anyone had ever put a whoopee cushion on my chair.) Still, Alma feared what would happen to her daughter if she died first.

If you are paying attention to the world you see a lot of pain.

I remember the tear-stained faces of two clients who on the surface couldn't have been more different from each other. Francesca was in therapy after a brutal date rape. SueAnne came because her husband had just killed himself. Francesca was a beautiful, dark-haired woman who ran the admissions program at a local university. Sophisticated and articulate, she could process her pain almost without my help. SueAnne was an extroverted redhead who answered telephones for a living. By nature she was a smart aleck, unaccustomed to discussing her private feelings. For months I saw SueAnne every Tuesday at 3:00 followed by Francesca at 4:00.

In their sessions they did much the same things. They cried. They raged. They worried about their kids. I will never forget Francesca's description of being thrown into a cement wall, having her teeth broken, of feeling cold and ready to die. I won't forget SueAnne's account of telling her five-year-old twins that their father was dead. One of them asked, "But he'll come home tomorrow, right?"

SueAnne and Francesca carried great burdens into my office, but like Alma, they made the best of their fates. In the end, they discovered that the terrible events had changed them forever, in sad ways, but in good ways, too. Francesca learned she was stronger than she thought. "If you can survive life, you can survive anything," she admitted.

SueAnne realized that she wasn't to blame for her husband's death, that whatever her failings were as a wife, ultimately her husband was responsible for his choices. And she discovered that sharing her feelings made them easier to bear. She left therapy a long time ago. I hope she remembers that lesson.

Most of the craziness in the world—violence, addictions, and frenetic activity—comes from running from pain. Many of the world's biggest bullies and worst mass murderers have acted to avoid confronting their own painful feelings. The only thing worse than feeling pain is not feeling pain. Healthy people face their pain. When they are sad, they cry. When they are angry, they acknowledge they are angry. They don't pretend to have only PG-rated feelings. They don't judge their feelings. Rather, they simply observe and describe them.

Of course, it isn't quite that simple. I have seen clients I simply could not comfort. For several months I worked with a woman who had been orphaned when she was very young. She desperately wanted nurturance, but she was so prickly that I could never make it through the hour without offending her. She left with all her pain undigested, angry with me for being one more person who let her down.

My definition of a healthy person is one who can grow and learn from all experiences. As an old man who had lost his wife, a son, and a daughter, poet Robert Frost said that he could sum up everything he knew about life in three words, "It goes on."

My hero is my Aunt Grace, who was in her eighties with an ill husband when her son died while mowing her lawn. By the time I called her, she had already organized herself mentally. She told me, "We'll just have to love and take care of the ones who are left."

Laura, this is not to say that the learning justifies the suffering. My heart ached for Lorena, Francesca, and SueAnne. But, helped by tincture of time, they all found what they needed to heal.

I hope this letter inspires you to go see the cranes. Standing on the bridge, as the cranes settled in, we shivered and stomped our feet to fight the chill. After a tangerine sunset, a half moon shone down on the Platte, its reflection spotlighting the black island of birds. The wind blew through the cottonwoods. We listened as the cranes tucked each other in with their soft murmuring. Our faces ached with the cold. But later, driving home in our warm car, sharing cheese sandwiches and apples, we felt happy, whole, and re-connected to Mother Earth.

8
■ Happiness

April 14

Dear Laura,

April is my favorite time to visit the Ozarks—the morel mushrooms are sprouting, the bass are biting, and the pink and white dogwoods cover the hills like giant gumdrops. As always I spend Saturday night at the Old-field Opry. This is a free show, housed in its own auditorium, that features old-fashioned country music, cornball comedy, and clog dancers aged five to ninety-five. Family and friends of the musicians serve the crowds chilidogs, chips, and the best raisin pie in the nation.

My cousin Steve is a founding member of the Opry, which has been going on for years. His close friend, Johnny Walker, sings and tells jokes, many of them about my cousin, whom he calls "Smilin' Steve." Johnny and Steve played together in rock-and-roll bands thirty years ago in high school. Johnny has a degenerative disease and is now on oxygen, almost blind, and paralyzed from the neck down. He spends a great deal of time in the hospital battling respiratory infections, but whenever he can make it, Johnny is on the Opry stage. His dad dresses him in his country western clothes and cowboy boots and helps the musicians carry him to his chair. Johnny welcomes the crowd and emcees the event.

Unable to move and losing his speech, Johnny has built a life that centers on music, but also involves a kind of Ozark Mountain counseling. Many people come by his house to talk. They leave feeling better, thinking that if Johnny can cheerfully handle his life, surely they can buck up and cope with theirs.

Johnny is living proof of what research shows: Happiness bears almost no relationship to good fortune. Rich people are not happier than poor ones. We humans tend to maintain a set point of happiness, staying at about the same level of happy or sad regardless of circumstances. Winning the lottery or having a cancer diagnosis changes this happiness quotient for only a very short time. As my Uncle Otis put it, "Most people are about as happy as they make up their minds to be."

Research documents that the more time people spend with other people, the better they feel. Friends play a critical role in well-being. Surprisingly, men and women are equally happy. On the surface this finding contradicts research that shows women report more depression. However, women also report more joy. They are more intense than men about all of their emotional states.

As a group, married people are happier than single ones; religious people are happier than nonreligious ones; and people working toward goals report greater happiness than drifters. In fact, people enjoy the process of working toward goals even more than they do reaching them. Freud once described a man as "wrecked by success." I've noticed a funny kind of sorrow and emptiness in people who have met all their goals. Unless they can redefine new goals that are meaningful to them, they are lost.

I often suggest to depressed clients that they volunteer at a soup kitchen. They perk up and feel luckier. I once arranged for a rebellious, lonely teenage girl to work at a rest home. Garnett was too stubborn to assist the cooperative patients the nurses recommended. Instead she chose Mr. Bottler, a mean-spirited and cantankerous octogenarian. For several weeks, Garnett assaulted him with her idiosyncratic methods of bonding—loud MTV viewing, offers to paint his fingernails black, gifts of *Rolling Stone* magazines, and her favorite food, peanut butter and dill pickle roll ups. At first, the old guy begged the nurses to get rid of her. They tried, but Garnett kept slipping in. Finally, after a battle of the Titans, Mr. Bottler caved and talked to Garnett. She talked back and, almost in spite of themselves, the two became friends. My work was just beginning with Garnett, but this victory was a start.

One of the best things you can do for clients is encourage them to develop a good set of routines. These could include activities such as meditation, massages, and exercise. Walking the family beagle, buying a cup of coffee on the way to work, lunch by a fountain, afternoon tea with a loved one, a weekly jog with friends, a monthly visit to grandparents, a yearly reunion with old teammates, or a backpacking trip to the mountains. These rituals give people something to anticipate.

Ted Kooser's book *Local Wonders* begins with an old Bohemian proverb, "When God wishes to rejoice the heart of a poor man, He makes him lose his donkey and find it again." But, satisfying lives are about much more than the absence of tragedy. They are about appreciating what we have. Poet Bill Kloefkorn says, "Happiness is what finds you when you are loafing up to your potential."

I teach clients that there are many kinds of love. It's important to love more than one person, and to have good friends and close connections to neighbors, family, and friends. I caution, "Don't have just one hobby or way of making a living. Like a good stock portfolio, be diversified." Happiness comes from making good choices. Integrity, energy, perseverance, and courage all contribute. In short, happiness is related to character structure, work, health, and relationships.

Laura, most people might read this and say, "I know that already." But in fact, our culture constantly misleads us about happiness, and we psychologists have sometimes been a part of the miseducation. Especially in the 1960s and 1970s therapists encouraged a shallow definition of happiness that was essentially, "You'll be happy if you do your own thing."

Now we can be counterculture and recommend that clients seek contentment, an underappreciated goal, rather than bliss. Although bliss is great when you can get it, contentment is more achievable. We can pitch old pleasures—stories around fires, shared meals, good books, and beautiful music, whether it's African drums or Bach concertos.

When I think about happiness I imagine Johnny Walker all dressed up on the Opry stage, temporarily off his oxygen, but with his shiny canister nearby. He is poking fun at Steve and has the crowd and the musicians laughing. He is delicately soliciting donations for people whose houses have burned down or who have sick kids and no health insurance. I picture him with his eyes shut, nodding his head and smiling to "Orange Blossom Special" and afterward smacking his lips as his mother feeds him a piece of homemade raisin pie.

9
Metaphor

April 16

Dear Laura,

Last night an unseasonable blizzard blew into Lincoln. The day before the temperatures had soared into the fifties and the sky glistened robin's egg blue. As I cut grasses and raked, I could hear geese moving north in their sinuous Vs and a cardinal in my crabapple tree. But this morning I can only hear a crow cawing. We'll have to relocate our snow shovel.

Spring is hope, birth, and the return of joy. All humans, not just poets, are metaphor-generating creatures. My dad referred to rich people as, "prosperous as Baptist bootleggers." My Aunt Margaret called television, "Manure garnished with parsley." My neighbor once described his son, who was preternaturally lucky, as, "Falling in a bucket of pig slop and coming out wearing a new suit."

Nietzsche wrote, "Truth is a mobile army of metaphors." Good therapists keep a toolbox filled with well-polished metaphors. Life can be compared to a book, a dance, a journey, a day, a pop quiz, a song, climbing a ladder, a feast, a jail sentence, or a garden. In my opinion, life is best not likened to war or sports, much overused comparisons that distort our worldviews. They frame life as competitive, violent, and about winning and losing. While partly true, it's not the most helpful way to frame the human experience.

From the beginning, I used the metaphor of a cut finger to discuss the importance of allowing oneself to experience feelings. I would say to a middle-aged banker ashamed of his tears, "If you cut your finger it bleeds. You may not like blood, but it is the way healthy bodies deal with wounds." When talking to a high achieving but unhappy professor, I might say, "You can get all A's and still flunk life." To an executive who is making half a million dollars a year but facing an angry family and sullen employees, I might steal Lily Tomlin's line, "You can win the rat race and still be a rat."

I tell a factory worker who lives with her brain-damaged father, "You are a flower in the desert. You only need a little rain to blossom into all your beauty. You're strong and self-reliant, but rain would help." To a person about to make a big mistake, I say, "If you jump off that cliff I'll stay in contact. We can have some great talks as you fall, but I can't stop you from crashing and burning at the bottom of the valley." Metaphors fall flat on their faces with some clients. Once, with a rather concrete thinker, I compared life to a journey. He responded by saying, "I can't afford a vacation this year." Refugees and others for whom English is a second or third language also easily get lost with metaphors. Even a metaphor as simple as "life is a bed of roses" can lead to question such as, "Do Americans sleep on flowers?".

Some of my metaphors are hokey or trite, but the best are like pebbles whose rough spots smooth down over the years. They grow rounder and more simply true.

I am thinking about your client's dream that he was in a canoe, pulled under water by a shark that held the towline in his teeth. You did a fine job analyzing that dream, which has the potential to be an extended metaphor. Your client is experiencing a rough patch right now, and his little boat is about to be pulled under in spite of his efforts to paddle. Metaphorically, he is surrounded by sharks. Solutions can be couched in terms such as, "You are managing to out-swim the sharks," or, "You see an island up ahead."

Dreams often provide economical metaphors. I'm no expert in dream work and I generally encourage clients to do their own interpretation. I invite them to speak for all the characters in their dreams. I ask how they feel about events in their dreams and what real-life events come to mind as they describe their feelings. Words spoken aloud in dreams are often deeply symbolic, and I suggest clients say them out loud and interpret them for me.

Natalie, an English major in her late twenties, hadn't found work or peer relationships that were sustaining. She had recurring dreams in which she couldn't walk. Sometimes the floors were covered in oil or glue. Other times, her legs were rubbery or paralyzed. Or, she was wearing iron boots or was tied to a stone. Often in her dreams she would shout, "I can't walk." This succinct metaphor became shorthand for us to discuss her situation. As Natalie found her way in life, her dreams reflected that progress. In fact, they were yardsticks for the distance she was moving toward her goals.

Another client, Arthur, was chronically ineffectual with an ever-growing pile of unpaid bills, parking tickets, and unanswered letters. He lost jobs, girlfriends, and car keys. He schlepped through his life, either pondering decisions too long or not at all. Opportunity not only passed him by, it ran circles around him. Arthur described himself as "a man with no hands." My assignment for Arthur was, "Keep a record of every time this week that you use your hands."

Seven-year-old Martha, a victim of sexual abuse in her family, called herself a broken teddy bear. She said, "My stuffing has fallen out. I'm dirty and no one wants me."

You know your metaphors are working when clients embellish them to describe their own experience. By the end of therapy, conversations may mostly be metaphorical. I can ask, "Did you work with your hands this week? Is your canoe above water?" Clients can say, "I had a dream of walking," or, "My teddy bear has new friends."

Families often select objects to represent them. The way these totemic items are treated is the way families treat themselves. Our neighbor's old cocker spaniel is half-blind, lame, and irritable. But he is admired, coddled, and much discussed, because he is who all family members love in common. Foods such as barbecue and pie are often metaphors for love. Recently I saw an older woman board a plane carrying an angel food cake with chocolate frosting. She held it on her lap for our cross-country flight. She told me, "This cake was baked with love."

Once I saw a family who discussed all issues—love, control, and distance—in terms of cars. We spent hours negotiating who could drive which car where. I wanted to shout, "Could you talk about something besides who washed the car on Sunday? Could you debate anything but your son's speeding?" I tried to direct the family into more important issues. Finally, I realized they were already there. The discussions about who drove what to work or who bought gas were about power, responsibility, and sharing. When these issues were properly resolved, family problems were solved.

When straightforward language starts arguments, or when language cannot touch what's most important, it's time to move to metaphors. Metaphors possess a fill-in-the-blank quality that allows for more creative responses.

As with all power tools, metaphors must be used carefully. Make sure they have the effect of lightening your clients' loads and making problems more manageable. Don't compare a harsh remark by an in-law to murder, compare it to a pebble in a sock. And keep your metaphors fresh. Dead words smell bad. Watch out and don't use the same metaphors too many times with the same clients. I actually keep notes on the metaphors I have used and the ones clients generate. Once I employed the "when you cut your finger it bleeds" metaphor twice, or maybe three times, with the same client. To my chagrin, she flashed me a look of impatience.

I never remember reading anything about metaphors when I was in graduate school, but over the years I have found them to be indispensable tools. My advice is look for your clients' metaphors and generate some of your own. Assign yourself the task of generating three metaphors a day. Borrow mine and turn to poets for more exquisite ones. Let me know how "the sinking canoe among sharks" works out for you.

I can see the snow melting from my study window. My crocuses, like Easter eggs, shimmer purple, yellow, and lavender against the snow. My eyes crave the daffodils' first salute. Flowers poking through snow answer Einstein's most important question, "Is the universe a friendly place or not?"

10
■ Endurance

April 20

Dear Laura,

Ugh! Last night I had another book-tour nightmare. I dreamt I was at an airport on my way to a speech and had forgotten my ticket. At first I wasn't too upset. That lapse could be remedied by telling the airline clerk my destination. But as I approached the desk, I couldn't remember where I was going. I was pawing through my briefcase looking for any scrap of paper that would enlighten me as to my destination. I woke up with my heart racing and the taste of metal in my mouth.

I am in the middle of a tour, home for Easter weekend. After weeks of flying from city to city, speeches every night and room-service meals, I am slowly putting my life back together. The taste of my own cooking delights me. I love writing books, but I don't much care for what I need to do to help sell them. There are two kinds of writers, extroverts and introverts. The extroverts relish the tours, but must bully themselves into their offices to write. The introverts love being alone at their desks, but dread the tours. Guess which category I am in?

Book tours are like going through your wedding day over and over again. Like a bride, a writer is surrounded by admirers in a way that is both stressful and exhilarating. Except unlike the bride, a writer is badly dressed, running late, jet lagged, and hungry.

From my point of view, it is no accident that "travel" and "travail" come from the same root word. I am not a road warrior and I grow anxious about everything—icy runways, lost luggage, car alarms in the middle of the night, and interviews with people who haven't read my books. But as Winston Churchill said, "When you are going through hell, keep going."

Humans encounter three kinds of problems. Problems like speech phobias or unruly children are usually solvable with information and effort. Others, such as eating disorders or entrenched marital problems, require sophisticated solutions. And finally there are problems that are simply not solvable—a child who will not reconcile with a loving family or the physical and mental health suffering of old-old age.

With the first kind of problem we therapists can often be motivators. ("Let's teach you how to do time-outs with your toddler and set up a star chart for rewarding good behavior.") With the second, we can be outside-the-box thinkers. ("Maybe if every time you are tempted to binge, you play some Chopin and think of every country in the world you would like to visit.") When you meet problem three, it's time for endurance training.

The capacity to tolerate pain and sorrow is an under-appreciated virtue. We teach our clients to process their pain, to ask for help, and to look for solutions—all appropriate lessons at times. But when things are truly hopeless, it is best to speak of other things. During the Great Depression, our great-aunts didn't discuss their flat pocketbooks and empty kitchen shelves. Explorers in the Antarctic need not mention that it's cold. When the ship is going down, passengers gain nothing by screaming, "We are all going to die."

In hard times, helpfulness, good cheer, dignity, and forbearance emerge as stellar virtues. When my grandmother was dying of cancer, I complimented her on her bravery and interest in others. She replied, "However I behave, I am going to die soon. Complaining won't stop the pain. I might as well have the satisfaction of handling this with dignity."

No virtue is absolute. Too much endurance in one family member allows others to be slackers and induces martyrdom. But we can encourage clients to assess a situation realistically, do what they can, and then accept what they cannot. That is really what AA's serenity prayer encourages. "God grant me the serenity to accept what I cannot change, the courage to change what I can, and the wisdom to know the difference."

Of course, Laura, many of our clients have much harder things to endure than book tours. Your client Dana comes home from her job in customer service to a difficult teenaged son and a brain-damaged mother who demands total attention. Caught between them, her whole life is customer service. You can encourage Dana to weep and to tell you her feelings. And you can give her tips on caring for herself. But mainly you'll be teaching her that, to quote Tennessee Williams, "We endure by enduring."

A man once asked Abe Lincoln what should be engraved on an honorary plaque for his office. The man wanted Lincoln to furnish words of wisdom that would be helpful in all circumstances. Lincoln thought about it for a while, then said, "This too shall pass."

11
■ Self-Care

Dear Laura,

This morning a colleague called to tell me he is leaving our profession. At first, Carl laughed and said he planned to open a bait shop. But then he said he was worn down. During sessions his mind wandered to his morning's conversation with the wife, what to have for lunch, and places to go fishing. He caught himself looking at his watch. Even though Carl has a Ph.D. in clinical psychology, he planned to mow lawns, shovel snow, and help people clean their gutters.

Carl isn't the first person I've known to bow out of our business. Most of us feel grateful we can be therapists, but every year some of us leave for something less intense. And there are some therapists who should leave and don't. They are burned out, but stay in the business due to inertia. I feel sorry for them and for their clients.

Talking to Carl reminded me I wanted to tell you some things about protecting yourself that no one told me when I was a graduate student. Taking care of yourself is partly a matter of practicing what you preach. It's hard to coach someone on quitting smoking if you reek of tobacco. You can't be a good parent or a good therapist if your message is, "Do what I say, not what I do."

Take care of your brain. Therapy is not work we can "phone in." Once I tried to do therapy after I'd been up all night at a concert in Kansas City. All day long, I stifled yawns and fought back nap attacks with caffeine and sugar. My clients that day didn't receive their money or their time's worth. Of course, everyone has nights of sick children or noisy neighbors. But we can avoid attending rock concerts on weeknights. My husband, Jim, says, "Never operate a chain saw or do psychotherapy without a good nights' sleep."

For every hour Charles Dickens wrote, he walked an hour. That's not practical for therapists, but we do need to move whenever we can. I have one colleague who chops wood after work and another who rides her horse daily.

Many of us are what Jung called "wounded healers." We have mental illness in our families or trauma in our own backgrounds. Certainly we can help others without being self-actualized, but if we're too needy, we don't have enough to give. I could fill a book with advice, but my thoughts can be summed up in three words—have a life. Have relationships and interests besides your work. Do things that make you laugh and recharge your batteries. Snuggle with a baby, take a cooking class, or join a theater group.

Because we spend our days talking and thinking, it's good to have off-hours filled with tactile pleasures. Yoga and meditation reconnect us with our bodies and relax tense muscles. Therapy is so damn ambiguous that we need to see a finished product now and then—a quilt, an oil painting, or a refinished oak desk. Jim often leaves the office and roars across town to the Zoo Bar where he jumps on the stage with his guitar and sings to a crowd that included the very people he has seen in his office that day. He lovingly refers to the Zoo Bar as the place where clients and therapists collide to boogie to the blues.

Being a psychotherapist is no Caribbean cruise with bonbons and bourbon. Daily we deal with suicidal clients, hassles with managed-care providers, and worries about abused and neglected children. For me the hardest work is being present when couples decide to divorce. Absorbing all of their pain absolutely wastes me. If we don't find good ways to cope with stress we will suffer from bad ways. So identify a half dozen things you can do to soothe yourself.

During my years in private practice, my office partners gave me advice and sympathy. If I needed to talk, they listened. Whenever I was too intense or anxious, they would figure out a way to get me laughing. We had weekly staff meetings and yearly retreats where we addressed big questions—Why are we doing this work? Do we still enjoy it? How could we do it better?

When Jim and I opened our practice we chose to limit the number of hours we worked. We saw ourselves as exhaustible resources, but resources that needed careful management in order to keep our therapy energy sustainable. We weren't big shoppers and could live on less money than many other people. We closed up the office when our kids had a swim meet or violin recital. We consistently valued time more than money and we were careful about selling our time.

I am definitely not recommending you do what we did. We've been teased about our clunky old furniture, see-through towels, and bargain-basement outfits. Most people don't like to drive cars with 150,000 miles on them. (Our luxuries have always been experiences, not products. We like restaurants, concerts, and vacations.) I am saying be intentional about what you do. Don't let your schedule just happen to you.

Hold to a reasonable number of clients per day. I found my limit to be six but I have known some therapists, tougher than I, who claimed they could do eight hours of therapy a day. Make sure you don't have too many DCs (difficult customers) on your caseload. Remember you always can say no. Don't let flattery seduce you into taking on a case when you are already full. Referral sources will press you to work more. They will cajole, "I don't trust anyone but you to handle this important case." If your caseload is full, the right response is "No, No, No."

Follow the code of ethics, to keep both your license and your sanity. Don't see anyone even remotely connected with your life outside therapy. Don't give your relatives IQ tests or administer a personality inventory to your cousin. Don't diagnose and label the neighbors. You aren't an expert with people you love. You can screw up a perfectly good friendship by being therapeutic.

Don't be persuaded into fulfilling inappropriate requests from clients. Don't meet clients for lunch, buy Amway products from them, or hire them to baby-sit or remodel your house. What makes the relationship so powerful is that there are no strings attached. So don't attach any.

Laura, this advice can be hard to follow. The only thing harder is not to follow it. The stakes are high in our work. Mistakes can cost lives. If we don't care for ourselves we can become as depressed, anxious, or angry as our clients. Please think carefully about how to protect, replenish, and enjoy yourself as a therapist. I don't want you selling bait and shoveling snow ten years from now.

12
■ Medication

Dear Laura,

I have been fighting the blues all week. It's hard to know what causes this. Sometimes it feels like sorrow over work struggles or a friend's sad news. Other times it seems as if I suffer from a kind of biological sludge that seeps into my good life and covers it with mud.

Did you know that spring is the season of suicides? No one knows why. It may be something biochemical, or it may be that if people are still unhappy with all this loveliness around, their depression feels inescapable.

It's not surprising that last week we disagreed about whether your client Marlene needed antidepressants. Some of our differences were theoretical and some felt more generational. I went to school in an era before there were good psychiatric medications and I was trained to see solutions in terms of the therapeutic relationships, not prescriptions. You are more of a biological determinist than I am. Mostly we discussed Marlene's case philosophically: Is she just sad because her boyfriend dumped her? When is medication appropriate? I laughed at your concluding remark, "Biology isn't destiny but it isn't chopped liver either."

If five therapists saw Marlene we would have six different theories about the cause of her sadness. Our field has always had competing notions about why humans act the way they do. Many earlier theories are stale now, but a thousand others, some very old, still flourish. Our theories range from biochemical, genetic, and environmental to spiritual and existential. We believe people can have trouble because they have certain kinds of brains or inborn temperaments, or because they are victims of childhood abuse, or members of an oppressed minority, or because of their birth order. We suggest misery is related to maladaptive behavior patterns, poor communication skills, irrational thinking, and a lack of meaning in life.

There is no doubt that some depression is biologically based, entrenched and relatively unrelated to the environment. I've seen clients who reminded me of Richard Corey. He was the healthy, loved, and successful man who killed himself in Edwin Arlington Robinson's well-known poem. One of my clients was so prone to despair that even good luck caused her dismay. She once opened a fortune cookie that read, "Money will fall from the sky for you." She shouted, "My god, I will be killed when it hits me on the head."

Much of what we call depression is simply sadness brought on by events. I think of Erin who had a dull, uncaring husband, a lousy job, and very little in her life that was fun or rewarding. I think of Amin who ran the gift shop at my hotel in Toronto. He had been a psychiatrist in his native country, but was unable to secure his license to practice in Canada. He told me proudly that he had once presented a paper at an international conference in the Azores. Now he spends his days selling breath mints and bottled water.

To quote old-time country singer Sam Morrow, "We need to be able to tell the difference between 'that's life' and 'that's nuts.'" One of our most important jobs is to help clients distinguish between depression and sorrow. The extremes are easy to call. Richard Corey might have been helped by antidepressants. Erin could benefit from a new job, some women friends, and a hobby. Amin needs a cultural broker to help him through the physician's credential system. It is cases such as Marlene's where we can really struggle to reach consensus. And her case is most likely not either/or but rather both/and.

Just as light can best be understood if it is considered as both a particle and a wave, mental health problems often are both biochemical and environmental. Furthermore, the factors interact with each other. Research demonstrates that reactions to circumstances engender permanent changes in the brain. Depressed people have different brains than nondepressed ones, but they also often have different lives. They jog less and attend fewer parties and picnics.

Bipolar disorder and schizophrenia are more easily managed if the client isn't homeless, fighting breast cancer, drinking heavily, or in an abusive relationship. Lifestyle factors and existential choices affect mental health just as they affect physical health. Virtually every disorder has many causes. What factors should we emphasize?

Our clients ask us why questions. "Why me? What's causing this?" We need to choose the most benign theory possible, that is, the theory that requires the fewest radical changes before they feel better. We don't want to blame their parents, their recovered memories, or their chromosomes. We want to frame their situations with a theory that leads them toward good decisions.

What we tell Marlene will influence what she does, how she sees herself, and how others will see her. Being labeled depressed is a mixed blessing. It can help Marlene obtain support, but it may make her feel that her happiness is beyond her control. And the label may cause others to write her off as unreliable and hopeless. So as of this morning, here's what I think we should do.

Let's assume that Marlene is dealing with a combination of sadness, stemming from her breakup with her boyfriend, and depression. We will give her a month to fight the depression without medications. Meanwhile you can obtain more information about her family history, her relationships, her sleep, and alcohol and drug use. You can initiate Be-Good-to-Marlene homework. Make sure that every day she is seeing people who care about her. Encourage her to watch fun movies, luxuriate in bubble baths, and listen to soft music. Recommend exercise, the more the better. Ask her to write down things she feels proud of. Teach her to take mini-vacations, little breaks that allow her time to savor moments. Talk through issues that are troubling her. Let's see how much she recovers. In a month if Marlene isn't significantly better, we will consider medications.

In the meantime, come by my house and we will debate these issues some more. I could use a good walk, a treatment that works for both depression and sorrow, and makes supervision sessions a great pleasure.

13
■ **Dating**

May 21

Dear Laura,

Did you ever hear the old country song with the stinger, "I am so miserable without you that it's almost like having you here"?

Last night a friend and I drank limeades and talked about her new boyfriend. Cora is intelligent, stable, and sophisticated. But when she discusses dating, she looks like a frightened child.

Cora married years ago when she was in medical school. After three painful years, she was divorced. About her marriage she said sadly, "I was young and I wasn't good at asking for what I wanted. I took too many things personally. The older I get the more I realize that most of what other people do isn't about me."

After her divorce she avoided close relationships with men. Only since the tragedy of September 11 has her need for support outweighed her fears of being hurt. Three months ago Cora met Arnie at a singles dance at her church. He's a general contractor, personable and hardworking. Cora is trying to get a handle on her new relationship. She doesn't want to settle for a man not worthy of her love, but she doesn't want to be too picky either. She sighed, "I don't think my criteria are all that high—I want an interesting, employed, moral, nonaddicted, and nonattached heterosexual. But I'm not finding droves of men who qualify."

Cora and Arnie generally have fun on dates. She's a liberal and he is conservative, but they laugh about their political differences. However, she frets that Arnie doesn't always do what he says he will do. He isn't very self-disclosing and, when she talks about her feelings, he changes the subject. I warned her, "Ninety-nine percent of all women say that men don't know squat about dealing with women's emotions." She laughed and admitted, "I've never met anyone in that one percent."

As she left my house, Cora confided, "I envy my sister. I don't want to be a housewife in Humansville, Missouri, but she doesn't have to put on expensive, uncomfortable clothes and try to be hip."

With dating, Cora is entering an emotional minefield. Falling in love, having sex, and making commitments, in whatever order you take them, these things have always been risky. That is why throughout history, in all times and places, courtship behaviors have been heavily ritualized. But dating in America in the twenty-first century unhinges us all.

Cora's story reminded me of a hundred other stories from my work as a therapist. Even though she was a fun-loving charmer, Abby couldn't find anyone to love her. She was a CEO and men were intimidated by her power. Wally always picked women who treated him badly. Dean and Magenta dated for fourteen years, but could never commit to each other at the same time. After her father's death Shawna moved in with an abusive alcoholic. Marcia and Mitch had a caring relationship, except Mitch always had sexual partners on the side, which he called "play relationships."

In my era, dating was no walk in the park. I remember wrestling matches in backseats and arguments over below-the-neck touch. I recall the anxiety girls felt and the anger guys expressed during sexual negotiations. But it's worse today. There is more information about sex now, but there is also more pressure to be sexual and, of course, there is AIDS.

The rules for dating can be contradictory—be real but be cool, be sexy but not sex-obsessed, be charming but don't try too hard, and don't talk about expectations yet expect things to go smoothly. Everyone has hot cognitions—worries about being used or not being desired, fears of rejection or entrapment, and fears of abandonment or of being controlled. It is a rigged game but it's the only game in town. People must play in order to have families of their own. And if the game ends badly, people struggle to carry on with civility. The intensity of feeling about breakups overwhelms ordinary human instincts for continuity and kindness. Gentle people end up hating each other.

Television and movies exacerbate our problems. We see hundreds of images of gorgeous people flirting cleverly, then moving into graceful, gymnastic sex, without sweating, bad breath, or discussions about birth control. I remember a couple who came in with sexual problems. Helen was heavy and Bob watched lots of television. He pressured Helen to lose weight. She told him, "Give up. My family is full of fatties. No matter how much weight I lose, I'll never be Michelle Pfeiffer." Her words were bold, but Helen was hurt by his judgment and she feared being naked in front of him.

I encouraged this couple to take walks in the evenings after dinner. This would have them physically active together in a setting away from the TV. Bob groaned over that idea, but he was willing to sign up for a gym so that they could work out together. Helen agreed, mostly just to spend time with her husband away from the television. Later, she grew to relish the workouts. Helen never lost much weight, but as we talked through relationship issues, her weight became less important to Bob. He wanted her fit, which she was indeed becoming. And he appreciated her other fine qualities. As he put it, "Hell, she puts up with me."

An already murky and perilous situation can be torpedoed by gender differences. Men are taught that real men don't express feelings—except for anger and lust. They learn that if they are too nice, women will walk all over them. Women are taught to flirt, but also to play hard to get, without being a tease. Meanwhile, women yearn for a romantic hero who washes dishes and whispers, "I love you," while men fear being too open about their feelings unless they are sexual feelings. Women tremble asking for commitment and men worry they'll be considered wimps if they take out the trash or admit they are in love.

There is one interesting exception. Men are allowed to express feelings in their art. Take music, for example. Off stage, cool musicians are laid-back, low-key, even taciturn. But oddly, on stage, the "coolest men" break our hearts with every song. Chet Baker's music was filled with pain and yearning, while his off stage manners were those of a cool hipster. George Jones, Joe Cocker, Van Morrison, B. B. King, and the Everly Brothers all sing as if relationships were matters of life and death. Their voices tremble, groan, crack, and roar with emotion. All the emotions that cannot be expressed by men in real life are expressed in songs. On stage, it's okay to have feelings. Off stage, it's important to be macho.

Teenagers receive more lessons on driving a car than on dating and making relationships work. Once I asked a college student how she decided to get involved sexually. She answered, "I don't know. I just get drunk and do it." A fraternity boy on a campus I visited was arrested for the date rape of a coed while he was on the phone ordering her "morning after" flowers. The night before, he had what he thought was consensual sex. But his date was horrified that he didn't understand that "'No' means 'no.'" She had reported a rape to campus police when she returned to her dorm.

Many people marry to escape the roller-coaster ride that is dating, which is right up there with foot-binding and burning witches at the stake for painful, misguided cultural customs. Although, to mix metaphors, many people jump from the roller coaster into the fire.

Laura, warn your clients that all that glitters is not marriage material. To evaluate another person, it's necessary to see them in many settings. Encourage your clients to meet their dates' family and friends and to be wary of anyone who has no family and friends. Tell women to listen to how men talk about other women and watch how they treat their mothers. Pay attention to how a date describes past relationships. Blamers are not good relationship risks. Neither are jealous, secretive, or controlling people. Dates who push boundaries and don't respect limits are likely to be bullies as time unfurls. Too much intensity too early also bodes ill. Stable people go slowly.

I'm not much of a romantic. I have less trust for being in love than I do for being good friends. I suggest clients pay attention to old-fashioned virtues such as respect, loyalty, stability, and honesty. The dating scene is not for the faint of heart. Tell your clients that, unlike in the movies, when they kiss, they should keep their eyes open.

PART III: SUMMER

14
■ Marriage

Dear Laura,

I just returned from my morning run—90 degrees and 90 percent humidity. June is Jim's band's busiest month. I feel for all the couples who have outdoor weddings this weekend.

Wedding ceremonies make me cry. One part of me wants to shout, "Have you thought this through?" Another part bursts into tears at all that vulnerability and hope.

Mark Twain wrote that marriage is an example of the triumph of faith over experience. Certainly on the day people marry, they feel deeply in love. But, over the years almost all marriages have serious crises, and half end in divorce. To quote another great writer, Jorge Luis Borges, "Love is a religion organized around a fallible god."

In the thirty years I've seen couples in therapy, some things change, some remain the same. In the Midwest in the 1970s, couples talked about sex. I did marital enrichment work that involved coaching staid Nebraskans to be creative, communicative, and lively in bed. I blush when I remember my sessions with people who expressed anxiety or boredom about the quality of their sex lives. I lectured them on foreplay, massage, and vibrators. I encouraged couples to make love in new places and in different positions. Oh, the seventies. . . it is hard to explain the sexual revolution to anyone from your generation.

In the 1980s couples argued about money and in the 1990s they fought over time. In our current decade, the challenges couples face involve the struggles from all three of the past decades. Everyone is so busy earning money that there is no time for sex or even conversation. As one client put it, "sleep is the new sex." But the age-old problems remain: How do you resolve conflict, make good decisions, and get along with the in-laws? How do you reconcile "we" with "I"? How do you have someone around when you want them around and not around when you don't? How do you make passion last?

Marriage is both natural and unnatural. Mating for life is cross-species behavior. But until recently, life was much shorter. Modern marriage requires two people, often with different interests, personal styles, ways of communicating, and habits, to live together for sixty years. People change enormously over those decades. As therapist Carl

Whitaker put it, "I have been married seven times—all to the same woman." Of course, if marriage partners don't change, that creates a different set of problems.

The worst marriages are the "can't live with and can't live without" kind, in which relationships are riddled with addictions, lies, and violence. A close second for worst place is the utterly disconnected couple, who shares space but nothing else. Both fire and ice suffice for destruction of the human soul.

Passionate but mercurial marriages thrive on fighting and making up. Taciturn, withdrawn couples eschew any discussion of conflicts. Over time, more and more things are left unsaid, until the sheer weight of unresolved issues breaks the back of the marriage. Often these couples divorce without ever having an argument.

In some marriages, one person calls all the shots. Most marriages have one person who is the pursued while the other mate is the pursuer, one eager-to-please partner married to a withholding person who likes being pleased. And we all know couples who could best be nicknamed the "Bickersons." In these couples, criticism and nagging are entangled with love.

A common dynamic for couples is that one mate is intellectual and controlled while the other is impulsive and emotional. Often, the man is the more detached and analytical one. Therapist Jan Zegers calls this the "stone and the witch syndrome." In time, this kind of marriage destabilizes. The emotional person feels she must shout louder and louder to get a reaction from a mate who grows more wooden and unresponsive. Over the years, these couples become caricatures, locked in roles no one would choose.

Contrasting personalities can benefit a marriage. Many relationships work because one person supplies the stability and the other the energy. As one happily married client put it, "I'm the gas. He's the brakes." Two over-controlled people married to each other are likely to have clean houses, balanced checkbooks, and well-organized schedules. But they may also be a little antiseptic and bland. Two florid emotional people are likely to burn each other up before year one is finished.

Too much contrast leaves people lonely. I remember a couple in which the wife was intuitive, empathic, and complicated. She was married to a computer programmer who sloughed through emotional and interpersonal issues. She was a loyal wife who stayed in the marriage for the kids. She did all the emotional work to make the marriage viable. But she felt pummeled by the husband's boorishness. She once said bitterly, "He is aggressively dull. He would be happy with anyone who liked to have sex and knew how to grill bratwurst." Of course, the husband felt unappreciated for being a solid citizen and a good provider. He also had stayed in the marriage for their children. Only duty connected this couple. And duty alone makes for bitterness.

There are truly happy marriages, but depending on your definitions, these can be rare or common. The closer I am to couples, the more I am aware of the fault lines in their relationships. On the other hand, happy doesn't mean perfect. A surprising number of people value their mates in spite of chronic unresolved issues.

Most marriages combine aspects of all the above relationships. I have always resisted classification schemes. Nobody is as simple as any category. Al and Carina are a case in point. Al came in wearing cowboy boots and tight, faded jeans. He made his living as an auctioneer at a stockyard. His wife, Carina, was a poufy-haired blond, a former barmaid, who said, "Now I work for Al." They came to see me because Carina was growing weary of her role as a big-hearted, good-time girl. What being a Waylon Jennings heroine meant was that she cleaned, cooked, and did laundry and yard work while Al hung out at the local honky-tonk.

During our first session, I had trouble connecting to this couple. Al raged about being in therapy and took it out on me. He called me Dr. Pipher, and thinking to soften things a bit, I invited him to "Please call me Mary, henceforth." He smirked and called me, "Mary Henceforth." When I raised my eyebrows, he shrugged and said mildly, "Lady, you asked for it." When I asked him to define his ideal marriage, he said, "The perfect woman would be a nymphomaniac who ran a liquor store."

What a defensive smart aleck! On the other hand, Carina struck me as smiling, sugary, and totally unable to stand up for herself. Her first words were, "My doctor sent us because of my acid stomach."

Of course, good therapy transcends first impressions. Al came from a family where his father slapped his mother around and charged her what little money she made selling eggs for a ride into town on Saturdays. Al's peer culture was men who believed in keeping women barefoot and pregnant. Given his background, Al had come a long way. He had never physically hurt Carina and he genuinely wanted her to have fun. He seemed almost puzzled that she wasn't satisfied with staying home in a nice house.

Carina also came from a home with a dominating father and a beaten-down mother. She had no models of assertive women, but she had managed to get Al to therapy and with my help she began to verbalize her complaints. They both identified good things about their marriage. Carina said, "Al would never cheat on me. And he's lucky with money."

Al winked at me, then said, "The harder I work, the luckier I get." I asked Al what he liked about the marriage. He smirked, "Carina is good in bed." Then he choked up and added, "She's my best friend. I don't know how she puts up with a jerk like me."

As to goals for therapy, they had only a few. Carina wanted Al home on Saturday and Sunday nights. During the week she wanted him to call by mid-afternoon if he wasn't going to be home for dinner. "That way," she said, "I'll microwave myself something and spend my time the way I want." Al said, "Carina is A-Okay." Then he paused, "Well maybe she could drop a couple of pounds." I groaned and Carina threw a Kleenex box at him. He laughed and said, "All right, All right. Forget I said that."

This couple's communication style was not what therapists would recommend. But they had modest expectations about marriage and after five sessions, they left pretty satisfied with each other.

Good communication doesn't mean saying everything. Lots of couples who communicate spend their time nagging, criticizing, and venting, none of which necessarily helps. Good manners soften hard hearts. Laughing together eases tension effectively. As Al and Carina's marriage shows, there are plenty of ways to make things work.

Happy spouses tend to see their partners as smarter, better looking, and sexier than they really are. Research shows that positive illusions about one's spouse foster good marriages. A man whose wife sees him as a hero is more likely to behave heroically. I apply this research to therapy by reinforcing positive statements about spouses and challenging negative ones. ("I agree with you completely that still waters run deep." Or, "What makes you think your husband doesn't love you?")

I knew a couple happily married for over fifty years. At their anniversary celebration, they were asked to reflect on their many years of married life. The wife said, "I regret the time we wasted trying to improve each other." The husband said, "The secret of my marital success is I wake up every morning, look in the mirror and say to myself 'You're no prize either.'"

Hope doesn't always die. There is often a depth of wisdom and emotion that comes from years of sticking it out. I think of my Aunt Agnes, small and frail, with severe osteoporosis. She cares for my large, wheelchair-bound uncle who is in his nineties. It is hard on her health, but as she puts it, she "wants to give him the gift of dying at home." That is a kind of love young people in their wedding finery cannot even imagine.

15
Helping Ophelia's Family

June 23

Dear Laura,

After you scheduled your first family-therapy case, you looked crazed as you asked me, "What do I do with all those people?" I promised I would write down some of my thoughts about family work.

Caution: Long Letter Ahead!

I faced my first family when I was an intern in Galveston, Texas. A team of students and supervisors watched me work from behind a one-way mirror. Because I had claimed to speak Spanish on my internship application, I was assigned to work with a Mexican mother and her five unruly kids. Alas, my Spanish was woefully inadequate for this overwhelmed, fast-talking mom. While I was catching maybe half of her story, the kids rocketed out of control. The youngest literally climbed the walls, shredding our curtains in the process. The supervision team alternated between phoning in instructions, which I was unable to execute, and laughing their behinds off at my ineptitude.

My second case, mercifully unobserved by the team, was a middle-class couple with a rebellious teenager. At the time I knew almost nothing practical about teenagers. But that didn't stop me from offering smug and mostly useless advice. In retrospect that couple was amazingly patient with me.

I can only recall one simple case. A young couple came in with their five-year-old daughter who suffered what used to be called night terrors. After a few questions, I discovered that she sat on her dad's lap every night as he watched the ten o'clock news. She loved snuggling with her dad, but I suspected the news was upsetting her. I advised the father to turn off the television and read bedtime stories instead. The girl's bad dreams disappeared. That case was a walk in the park—good parents, a normal kid, and a solvable problem.

My first years of family work overwhelmed me. My professional training seemed useless in the presence of real families. No lecture prepared me to handle a bitter wife who refused to talk in our session and her husband who showed up reeking of alcohol. Trying to talk about communication with that drunk guy and his sullen wife may have been my low-water mark as a therapist.

We must dance between the raindrops to do family work. Our job is to validate every point of view and, at the same time, stay out of trouble with other family members. There is an old joke about a rabbi doing marital therapy. First he listens as the wife pours out her heart. "Yes," he says, "Yes, you are right." Then the husband explains his side of the story. "Yes," the rabbi says, "You are right." The couple shouts at the rabbi. "You can't agree with both of us. We have totally different points of view." "Yes, yes," agrees the rabbi. "You are both right."

The most important work early on is understanding the family environment. You need to assess family resources, hot-button issues, and potential crisis points. Note strengths, virtues, talents, and signs of resiliency. Identify who in the family wants to change. Ask a teenager, "When you and your parents are again close, what will you want them to understand about this time in your life?" Ask members how they would know the family was solving its problems. Ask, "If you had a magic wand, what change would each of you make in this family?" It's amazing how simple most people's needs are— parents want an adolescent to eat dinner with them, or a son wants his dad to play ball with him, or a man wants his wife to give him a kiss when he comes home from work.

Educate families about developmental issues. Often the most therapeutic thing you can say to a parent is, "This is normal for a kid this age." Help families hold reasonable expectations, not only about developmental levels, but also about how well families actually do. Say,

"All families have arguments over who does the dishes."
Or, "Kids beg for treats on vacations. That's hard-wired."

Be flexible, Laura. When you make suggestions, use
words such as "experiment," "temporary," and "pretend." That keeps people from being too threatened by
changes. If you're in over your head, find a cotherapist.
Especially with teenagers, if therapy is not working, invite in grandparents. Adolescents may be furious at their
parents, but often they love and respect Nonna and
Papa. Eventually the number of people in the room
helps the teenager feel cared for and contained.

In a healthy family, people take turns being the needy
one, the strong one, or the joker. In troubled families,
these roles are set in stone. When this happens, people
feel trapped in a script they didn't consciously choose
and that doesn't allow them a full range for character development. Help the identified patient (IP) off the hot
seat. Being the sick one shouldn't be anyone's full-time
permanent job. On the other hand, give the perfect
members of the family permission to screw up now and
then.

Encourage new groupings in the family. If dad never
does anything alone with his delinquent son, have them
work together on a project. If the parents seldom go out
because they are afraid to leave Junior at home, ask them
to send him to his grandparents for a week. Sometimes
simply rearranging people frees up new energy. Invite
clients to change chairs and then ask them to speak to
one another as if they were other family members. This

simple technique builds empathy. It works especially well with adolescents and their parents who often think of each other as coming from alien solar systems.

Problems are never so terrible that they can't be joked about. I know a therapist with a great sense of humor. Once a teenager showed up wearing bright orange and purple slacks and he asked, "Do you know the definition of psychotic?" The family looked baffled and he pointed to the slacks. "Now that's what I call psycho."

I chuckled with the parents of a child I was testing for the gifted program who asked me in all earnestness, "How do you spell IQ?" I joke about my own failures. When my son was twelve, I pompously told him he could ask me anything he needed to know about sex, that I would always answer him honestly and directly. His immediate question was, "Did you and Dad have sex last night?" I yelled, "You can't ask me that."

Oust secrets. There are three kinds of family secrets: the ones that members hide from the world, the ones they hide from each other, and the ones they hide even from themselves. Families cannot be more honest with us than they are with themselves. If they are denying dad's sexual abuse or mom's drinking problems, we may not know about these things for a surprisingly long time.

Secrets are all about shame. As poet Adrienne Rich wrote, "That which is unspoken becomes unspeakable." Secrets are also about power. They define in-groups and out-groups. Often, family members justify secrets as protection. "We didn't want dad to be upset." However, secrets isolate and allow people to do destructive things. Secrets erode trust.

Support parental authority. Earlier in the last century, our culture was a pretty authoritarian place with lots of rules and expectations. Healthy families balanced out the rigidity of the culture with their gentleness, love of fun, and relative permissiveness. But over the last few decades, adult authority has eroded. This has created terrible problems for children and for their parents. I see signs of this daily. Just yesterday I was at a picnic with a toddler who behaved rudely to a family friend. His mother said to him, "Apologize to Tina. That wasn't polite." But before the toddler could speak, Tina said loudly, "That's all right," and gave him a hug. The boy learned that his rudeness didn't matter.

Teach conflict-resolution skills, face-saving techniques, and exit strategies. The most useful phrase for anyone in a family is "I apologize." A great deal of anger and sorrow can be eliminated if family members learn to say they are sorry. Keep in mind that men and women tend to have different meanings for the word, "sorry." Women find it easier to apologize because they see it as saying, "I am sorry I hurt your feelings or caused you pain." Men have a tougher time because they often see apologizing as saying, "I am eating shit."

Make sure positive change is recognized. Family members often behave heroically and no one notices. Assign parents to actively observe their children being good and to watch for the secret good deeds that their mates do for them. I once saw a couple who had trouble raising their foster children because they focused on tasks such as studies and cleaning the bedrooms. They were a caring couple but they saw life in terms of duty. After one session, I heard the dad suggest they stop for ice cream. I called them back in from the waiting room to congratulate the dad on his fun-loving spirit. Much to my surprise, he choked up and had tears in his eyes after my compliment.

Celebrate moments. In every moment of life the banal and the profound are as intermingled as salt and pepper. Catch the profound and show it to the family. Say to the father, "The look you gave your son shows me how deeply you care that he is happy." In most sessions, as in much of life, the rhythm is blah, blah, blah, then insight or sparkling moment. Or unfortunately, it's blah, blah, blah, disastrous moment. It's astonishing how quickly things can go seriously wrong or incredibly right. A colleague told me of working with an angry daughter who talked about all the messes she had created in her life, then abruptly quieted down. After a few moments of silence her mother said, "I'm thinking of the phrase, 'paint one-self into a corner.'" The girl looked shocked and said, "That's just what I was thinking, too." The therapist complimented the mother's great understanding and said, "I'll just leave you two alone to talk about this further."

Create a mellow room tone so that a sparkling moment can happen. Couples don't stay together because they agree on who does the dishes. Try not to get tangled up in detail and somehow lose track of the magic that connected them in the first place. Ask couples how they happened to fall in love. Not always, but usually, people go dreamy-eyed, soften their voices, and tell a good story. To find magic with teens and their parents, ask about births. That reminds everyone of the primal bonding experience and their long history.

Exude calmness. Even when you don't feel calm, learn to act calm. Anxiety, anger, and despair are infectious. Model emotional control. Families need ways to cope with intense emotions. Be a purveyor of hope. Family therapy can be intense, scary, and loud. Every human is extraordinarily complex and in families this complexity is logarithmic. But hope generally makes things better.

No matter what people say, families are the source of our greatest joys and greatest sorrows. Zorba the Greek called families, "the whole catastrophe." My own family kept me humble. I have tried my hardest and felt my most incompetent as a parent. And our kids certainly didn't think we were perfect. Once our son drew a picture of himself between Jim and me. In this picture he was tiny and we were giants. Under the drawing, he wrote, "She's a psychologist. He's a psychologist. And I am just an innocent little boy." Another time after a long day at work I came home with a migraine. My son repeatedly tried to talk to me, and I kept impatiently signaling that I needed my space. Finally, he handed me his allowance and asked, "If I pay you would you talk to me?"

When my kids were teenagers I often had the experience of seeing parents who were drug addicted, abusive, or philanderers, whose kids were more respectful and well-behaved than my own kids. Other times I would realize I was "helping" couples who were better parents than I was. I would be tempted to take notes on what they said for my own family's benefit.

Laura, because you aren't a parent yourself, there may be times you are uncertain about advice. Usually the best strategy is to share that uncertainty. Amazingly, families usually find that disarming and end up reassuring you.

Whew, this was a long letter. Families are unique, multilayered, and not what they seem. They speak in code. Problems are sometimes decades in the making. You don't have to fix everything overnight. For a while you will feel outnumbered and outsmarted. Offer what you can and let the family do their own healing work. Families have survived for thousands of years without therapists.

16
▓ Intentionality

July 7

Dear Laura,

It was fun to run into you at Farmers' Market last week. Did you like the music from Chile? Did you purchase that braided rug? Did you buy fresh cherries or apricots? We have so many choices at the market, all of them good.

I wish we had more time to discuss the family you saw last week. I awoke remembering your line, "They are making all the wrong choices." Years ago I had a similar case. Justin and Annie were court-ordered into therapy after they were arrested in a bar on the outskirts of town. They had left their toddler and three-year-old outside in their pick-up while they partied. Partying is my least favorite verb. It covers a multitude of stupidities and glosses over consequences. It's a word that, to quote

my Grandmother Glessie, "paints a shit pile purple."
Anyway, someone saw the kids sleeping in the back seat
and called the police. Annie and Justin were charged
with child neglect and the kids were placed in temporary
foster care. The couple was referred to me for alcohol
evaluations and counseling.

Justin slouched in wearing a torn Aerosmith T-shirt,
black jeans, and engineer boots. Annie had spiky
tomato-red hair, a nose ring, and freckles. She wore
boots and jeans with a halter-top that would have been
sexy if she hadn't weighed 100 pounds. Her first words
to me were, "You look like my mom."

I was surprised how much I liked this couple. Justin
had a shy sweet manner and was eager to please. He had-
n't had a drink since the night they lost the children. He
swore he only drank as much as his friends, but he admitted, "That don't matter now. I want the kids back."

Annie claimed she didn't even like the taste of alcohol and that night had only sipped on a margarita. She
protested weakly that she'd checked on the children
every half an hour that night. She and Justin couldn't afford a baby-sitter and almost never went out. Just this
one time to celebrate Justin's birthday, they thought it
would be okay. But she choked up, "I can't sleep without
my babies."

Justin worked at a place that manufactured fertilizer
tanks and Annie cashiered at a convenience shop. They
had different shifts so they could save money on daycare.
However, that meant they were always exhausted and

rarely together. The baby had been born prematurely and they owed the hospital over $3,000 for their co-pay. But Justin had purchased an all-terrain vehicle and a deer rifle. He bought Annie her leather boots and designer jeans. They had a satellite dish and surround-sound TV, but not enough money for the baby's formula.

Justin and Annie had been educated by advertisers. Happiness meant owning the right stuff—big-screen TVs, cell phones, DVDs, and shopping-channel jewelry. They had been educated to consume brand-name sugar, caffeine, tobacco, and booze. Glitzy casinos lured them in. Credit card companies led them down a primrose path toward bankruptcy.

Fortunate children have parents who help them sort through the avalanche of choices. But Justin's dad was an alcoholic, in and out of jail, and his mother had abandoned him to a series of foster homes. He recalled carrying an empty lunch box to school every day and slipping off alone to pretend to eat lunch. Afternoons he worried that other kids would hear his stomach growl. Annie never knew her father and her mom worked two jobs. Neither of them had ever experienced family dinners or vacations. Justin and Annie loved their kids, but they were just kids themselves with little sense of how the world worked.

At the end of our first session, I asked if they wanted to return. They both nodded solemnly. I gave them a phone number for a Parent Training course and said,

"Next time bring your bank statement and we'll work on budgeting your money. You may have to sell some things to get your bills squared away."

Justin looked a little blue about budgeting, but he said politely, "Doc, you're calling the shots."

You won't be shocked to hear that Justin and Annie never joined Audubon or the PTA but they did get their kids back and their finances under control. They cut up their credit cards, always a step in the right direction. Instead of watching video games, Justin played a little ball with his older son. Annie started using time-outs to discipline the kids. They even turned off the television during meals.

I ran into them recently at a street dance, kids in tow. Annie had henna paintings on her arms and her hair was the color of cranberries. They were drinking sodas and the kids were giggling at their balloon animals.

This family happened to be low-income, but in my experience, the worst cases of runaway consumption appear in wealthy families who are avalanched by all their stuff. Unless they throw some of it away and talk to each other, nobody actually knows anybody.

Almost all families need help sorting out their relationships to time and money. Most of us cannot have both. A good assignment is to ask families to come up with their own definitions of wealth. Mine is the number of days a year I see my own adult children. For your clients, it might be the number of nights they have a family meal or the number of times a day the family laughs and has fun together.

Especially in the last decade, my main work is treating people's schedules. I help parents carve out a dinner hour or a family day. I encourage parents to set limits on activities. I teach that time, like money, should be allocated in keeping with values and priorities.

Stephan Rechtschaffen's work comes in handy. In his book, *Timeshifting*, he tells of seeing a bumper sticker, "Having a good time, wish I were here." He notes that Americans are always living in the future and that even when we can slow down and relax we often don't shift out of high speed. He teaches the present is the present and that if you live in the moment there is no stress. We can't do it all the time, but we can time-shift into a more relaxing pace some of the time.

Family rituals strengthen families. One of my favorites is the high-low report at dinner, in which everyone at the table tells about the best and worst thing that happened that day. Goodbye and hello hugs, music lessons, games of Cranium, and bed talks build protective walls around the family. I know of one family who walks around their neighborhood every night after supper, checking on their neighbors, the flora, and the fauna. The three things adults remember with the greatest pleasure from their childhoods are family meals, time outdoors, and family vacations. So, Laura, encourage your families to eat together, go on vacations, and spend time in the natural world.

Good parents are antidotes to advertising. They teach, "You are not the center of the universe." And they teach the meaning of "enough." Parents are the people who help children build meaning from all the complex information they are bombarded with daily. Especially with young children, it is important to keep the information they are expected to absorb relatively simple. My niece has a phrase she uses when her mother explains too much at once, "TMI, Mom." TMI stands for too much information.

Plato said education is teaching our children to find pleasure in the right things. We live in a culture that teaches us to love all the wrong things. If we don't interact very intentionally with the broader culture we end up unhealthy, stressed, addicted, and broke. I hope you can help your clients find good things to love. Have they been to Farmer's Market?

17
■ Emotional Weather

August 17

Hi, Laura.

I hope you are having a great time at Lake Okoboji. We vacationed there when our kids were small. There is nothing like a beach for children. But graduate students do well on beaches, too.

You missed an incredible day in Nebraska. Yesterday morning was blue and calm. By noon it was ninety degrees, gray, and windy. Henry James, no doubt under the influence of a balmy, blossom-filled day in the country, said the most beautiful phrase in the English language was "summer afternoon." He never visited Nebraska. Late afternoon black clouds rolled in. The sky turned greenish and a tornado formed south of town. The temperature dropped forty degrees in two hours and pea-sized hail peppered our lawn. But by sunset the sky was again clear and a full moon rose over yards filled with hailstones. Even experiencing it firsthand, I could hardly believe all that weather happened on the same day.

There's Nebraska weather with its highs of 110 and lows of 30 below zero and there's Los Angeles weather. My son, who lived in Los Angeles for a while, said, "We laugh at the weather forecasts. It's always partly sunny. The temperature only changes by a few degrees."

Places have different ranges of weather, and so do humans. In intensity of feelings and mood swings, we are not created equal. There are people who cope daily with the equivalent of tornadoes, while others bask in perpetual ocean breezes.

The most extreme emotional weather is bipolar disorder, in which every day people oscillate between elation and grief. Slightly less extreme weather plagued my client Maggie, who laughed and cried every session. What she loved, she loved so much it made her heart swell. What tickled her made her laugh until her sides hurt. On the other hand, the smallest slight caused her to sob in despair. She was often adrift on a heaving sea of emotions. Once she wailed, "I have mixed feelings about everything." Another time Maggie said to me, "You have no idea how many ups and downs have ravaged me in the last twenty-four hours."

In contrast, my friend Raymond is always relaxed and sanguine. When he told me about his mother's death, I was more emotional than he was. Dorothy Parker once described a man similar to Raymond derisively, "His emotions ran the gamut from A to B."

The weather in both Nebraska and Los Angeles has its virtues. Many creative people, who have intense and changeable moods, are exciting and popular. They are generally warm-hearted, enthusiastic, and effusive—all virtues if not carried too far. But they can also be high maintenance and their partners often report weariness with their storm-tossed charm. Folks with Los Angeles weather are reliable and steady as rocks. However, they can be dull as rocks, too. Their forbearance can stabilize their more emotional partners, or it can put them to sleep.

In therapy we are more likely to see people with Nebraska weather. They come to us because they need help repairing the damage from all those storms. They need stress-management skills and training in learned optimism and emotional intelligence. They are more likely to have trouble with addictions because they often seek chemical help in the hope of controlling the turbulence. (As Tom Waits put it, "I'd rather have a bottle in front of me than a frontal lobotomy.")

When the Los Angelenos are in therapy it's often because someone else wants them to feel something. With them our job is to create a little storm system and then teach them to describe it in an interesting way. We want them to pay attention to their feelings and not to respond to all questions about their emotional states by saying, "I am fine."

We could speculate on ideal emotional weather. However, just as with real weather, people have different preferences. Some people like flamboyant poets, others staid engineers.

I would pick someplace to live with weather like Boulder. Nestled between the mountains and the plains, it has four seasons, but none of them falls too harshly on its residents. The snow is generally light and doesn't last long. Summer days blister, but it cools down at night. Most of the time, the climate is right for all kinds of activities. I have a few Boulder-esque friends whom I deeply appreciate. They are exciting, yet stable.

Anyway, today in Nebraska, it's breezy and seventy degrees, Los Angeles weather. I will like it for a while, then I'll want something more exciting. Now what does that say about me?

18
Swimming

August 28

Dear Laura,

I just got back from my afternoon swim. The thermometer by the bank read 101 degrees. On a day like this, what else can one do but swim? Generally I swim ten laps, then read in the sun for fifteen minutes, usually the *New Yorker*, although right now I am reading Caro's *Master of the Senate*, a great summer book. Then I dive back in. The contrast between languor and movement, hot and cool, sun and water is refreshing and soothing.

The longer I live the more I respect swimming. As a kid, I spent my summers in the chlorinous pool in Beaver City. The pool opened at 1:00 and closed at 9:00 and often I was there all eight hours, splashing, bobbing, tanning, and eating Mounds bars and Popsicles for sustenance. Words cannot describe what a swimming pool meant to us in a little farming town in Nebraska in the 1950s. By August my body was cocoa brown and itchy, and my blond hair glistened a slimy green.

In junior high my son was an extroverted comedian. "I enjoyed school and school enjoyed me," he said years later. But in high school he swam laps four or five hours a day and eventually became a state champion swimmer. By now, many competitive swimmers wear underwater headphones and listen to music while they swim. But Zeke didn't have anything but his own mind to keep him occupied. What swimming gave him, as a testosterone-filled adolescent, was four hours a day to think. In fact, swimming laps, there was nothing to do but think. It deepened him as it did other serious swimmers from his era.

Swimming helps people of all ages. Kids bliss out by water, whether it is an ocean beach, a muddy creek, or a swim tub in the backyard. I have been at the YWCA pool when the arthritis class gathers. Elderly people walk gingerly into the pool area, wincing as they go down the ladders and shivering in the tepid water. But after an hour of water aerobics they are talking and joking. Their pain abates and, when they leave the pool, they move more easily.

Swimming relaxes, massages, and awakens punished bodies. It is therapy for anxious and depressed people, and people with health problems and chronic pain. When I wrote the book on refugees, I befriended many traumatized people. Often I gave them swim passes.

Many reported that swimming was the best thing in their lives. The rush of endorphins and the sensual, soothing nature of swimming helped them heal.

I took up swimming after a physical therapist told me my stress-induced back pain would disappear if I swam. She was right. By now, I am totally hooked. I love the wake up of the splash, the caress of the water, and the way my muscles warm as I proceed. And, as I do these good physical things, I give myself underwater therapy. As I paddle my version of the breaststroke and crawl, I review all the significant events since my last swim. I revisit tense interactions and reexamine the way I solved thorny problems. I re-enjoy the happiest events. I rehearse my lines for upcoming difficult conversations. When I emerge from the water I am healthier mentally and physically. I feel the way a person might feel after jogging, meditating, and then receiving a great massage.

Of course, swimming isn't for everybody. Other people quilt or play tennis or golf. You may find something equally calming for you and your clients, although, I don't think anything beats swimming. Swimming is primordial. We are made of water, once long ago we lived in water, and with swimming we return to water.

19
■ Danger

September 2

Dear Laura,

This morning there is an end-of-summer feeling in the air. Birds are clumping up on the wires. Marching-band music from a nearby high school blares through my study window. The asters, sunflowers, and surprise lilies bloom in the gardens. Last night I walked on Holmes Dam. For a long time, I watched a red fox stalk mice in the yellow grasses.

I've been pondering your question, "What do you wish you had learned in school?" During my five years of Ph.D. training, I listened to lectures on brain anatomy, the philosophy of science, schizophrenia, and the bene-fits of community programs. I learned how to induce trances, interpret responses to inkblots, and write a report. But nobody warned me that unless I was careful, and even if I was careful, I might get hurt.

In my graduate-school days I heard only one mention of danger—from a social worker who had several bones broken by a delinquent teenager. Bandaged from top to toe, she wryly admonished me, "Never get between an out-of-control adolescent and the door."

A few years ago, I attended a standing-room-only workshop on violence. The presenter asked people in the room who had been assaulted by clients to raise their hands. Two-thirds of the room did so. Then he asked people to again raise their hands if they had required medical care because of a client's assault. A hundred therapists in our small, relatively safe state had been seriously hurt by their clients or their clients' relatives.

It makes sense that therapists would be victims of violence. We deal with alcoholics, people with anger-control problems, psychopaths, people in crises, and the seriously mentally ill. We testify in custody and commitment hearings. We report child abuse and neglect. If teenagers are about to kill themselves or someone else, we tell their parents. We counsel gang members, methamphetamine addicts, and paranoid gun owners. We see people referred by employers because they scare their coworkers. Doctors, schoolteachers, family members, and employers send us their out-of-control people.

Generally therapists have no training in self-defense. Most offices do not have police or security. Many therapists work alone and some do home visits to people they have never met. One of my former students had a placement in an East Coast city that involved working nights at a walk-in drug treatment program in a rough neighborhood. She was lucky she wasn't killed.

In my practice I don't see many clients who are court-ordered into therapy and, if I can spot them in time, I turn down sociopathic clients. That is a luxury most therapists don't have. Still, over the years, I've had my share of menacing phone calls and people threatening to hurt me. There have been times when I was grateful that my home address and phone number were unpublished. I recall the Christmas I was pondering a death threat by a stalker who I'd worked with briefly. I cried as I watched my five-year-old daughter play carols with other Suzuki violinists in the brightly lit lobby of a bank. She and her friends looked so innocent and vulnerable. Outside snow turned our city dark and cold.

Part of being safe is being judicious in what we say in sessions, although this is a complicated issue. Sometimes we have an ethical responsibility to tell clients to do things that may put us in danger. We may have to insist clients protect their children from sexually abusive relatives by calling the police. In general, however, our job is not to tell people what to do. We present choices, clarify issues, and help people predict their own futures. But, we can't control how we are quoted outside our sessions. Many clients tell their families that we said they should do something that they wanted to do. Only, unfortunately, the clients hadn't the courage to own their decisions.

I once held a session with a woman who spoke bitterly about her mate and, at the end of the hour, announced she would seek a divorce. I encouraged her to slow down and consider marital therapy. But she drove home and told her husband that I had advised her to seek an immediate separation. The next day her husband called, swore at me for a while, then threatened to beat me up. Fortunately, I was able to talk him down.

Many therapists don't discuss scary incidents with their colleagues because they fear they will be blamed for mishandling things. That is a big mistake. Have an office plan for danger. Talk with your colleagues about how you can signal each other if something alarming happens during a session. Take a self-defense course. Keep your home phone and address private. Don't talk about your personal life in sessions and don't have family pictures and other mementos on display. Don't box clients in figuratively or literally. People who feel trapped can be dangerous.

If a client scares you, respect that feeling. If a situation feels unsafe, don't go into it; if you already are in, exit quickly and cautiously. You have a responsibility to assess for danger constantly, not only for yourself, but also for your clients and for other people involved in the case. If there are risks, do what must be done to protect everyone—have an extra therapist in the room, consult with attorneys, or call the police.

Laura, this letter is not meant to frighten you. It's really an ounce-of-prevention letter. Our field tends to be in denial about danger. For the most part, therapists are gentle, trusting people who find it hard to believe anyone would hurt them. But forewarned is forearmed. I don't want you to lie awake nights trembling like a mouse stalked by a red fox.

20
■ Therapy and Writing

September 11

Capetown, South Africa

Dear Laura,

Last year on September 11 our daughter was in Capetown. Along with all our other fears, we worried about Sara. How would she make it home with her flight cancelled and perhaps a war or another terrorist attack on the way?

By coincidence, I am working in South Africa exactly one year later. I have driven through the glorious blooming prairie to the Cape of Good Hope. I hiked Table Mountain and felt its "tablecloth" of deep fog surround me. I toured the poor township of Langa and the District Six Museum, Capetown's version of the Holocaust

Museum. I visited Robben Island where Nelson Mandela was imprisoned for thirty years.

Today I have thought about last September 11 and my daughter. When Sara finally returned from South Africa, she was out of step with the rest of us. As a way to deal with her intense grief, I recommended that she write. I said, "For me writing is the best therapy. I don't know how people who don't write survive."

When you asked me recently which I liked most, writing or doing therapy, you stumped me. I felt like you were asking which of my kids I prefer. Still, I pondered your question, realizing how alike the two enterprises are. For many years, I wrote in the mornings and did therapy in the afternoon. Both jobs involve spending time in small rooms waiting for inspiration. And both possess a considerable amount of mumbo-jumbo. Writers and therapists enact rituals to induce trances in themselves. My trances involve desks and drinks. When I write, I drink coffee at my desk overlooking my garden. My desk has all kinds of pens, paper, and pencils to keep me going. When I do therapy, I have legal pads for taking notes and bottled water. I try to keep fresh flowers on both desks.

With either kind of work, ringing phones or headaches can ruin our concentration. At the end of the day our backsides hurt and we aren't sure if we've done anything lasting. We're a little shocked when we reemerge into the real world of traffic, our families, and the nightly news.

Poet William Carlos Williams wrote, "Catch an eyeful, catch an earful, and don't drop what you have caught." This advice to writers applies equally well to psychotherapists. The tools of our trade include our intuition, intelligence, warmth, and character structures. Both jobs are highly disciplined endeavors that involve posing questions and generating problems to solve. They require laborious excavating for emotional truths. Both kinds of work demand we use everything we've got all the time.

Writer Rosellen Brown offered succinct advice for writers—show up, pay attention, tell the truth, and don't be attached to results. That is not a bad set of rules for therapists either. Both writers and therapists walk a tightrope; we must give the work our all, and yet we must detach from success or failure. Otherwise, we try too hard. And trying too hard at therapy or writing is like trying too hard at sleeping, having an orgasm, or being liked. It doesn't work.

I studied four years as an undergraduate and five years as a graduate student to get my Ph.D. in clinical psychology, but I taught myself to write. Still, there is a sense in which all writers and therapists, no matter where they study, are self-taught. We learn by making and then correcting mistakes. Nobody is good in the beginning. After a decade of hard work, I felt that, both as a therapist and writer, I knew what I was doing most of the time. By then I had good habits and a sense for the process. But beyond this level of competence, I kept learning. People are peculiar and nothing ever happens twice.

Over time, competent writers and therapists develop a voice. Ideally this voice expresses one's best inner knowledge. Work done with a true voice looks natural and easy to observers. But most of us must struggle to find a voice that beams through all our work.

In writing and therapy nothing is more important than a likable guide. With Bill Moyers, Mary Oliver, or Molly Ivans, I'd enjoy a ride to the recycling center. With dull or unsavory characters, I would dread a trip to Paris. Great guides are humble, competent, kind, and calm. They emanate an unusual mix of innocence and sophistication. Most important of all, good guides are trustworthy and inspire others.

Therapy and writing both ask their subjects to react emotionally. After reading a good book, readers are changed. And truly great works, such as *War and Peace*, *Silent Spring*, and *The Good Earth* change the world forever. After a profound therapy session clients are willing to reexamine the way they live their lives. The rigid Catholic father says of his son's Buddhism, "The prayers of all good people are good prayers." The bitter husband says, "Maybe I haven't really seen my wife the way she truly is." The alcoholic thinks, "Perhaps I could have a better life if I gave up booze."

Both jobs require a certain amount of verbal cleverness, but glibness also can get in the way. Writing that is too elegant distracts the reader. And, believe it or not, I once saw a therapist demonstrate a fancy-schmancy technique while calling the client the wrong name. The client was not impressed.

Writers and therapists expose the unexposed. These whistleblower jobs are risky and punishing. We are subversives who commit the crime of telling the truth, often to people who have deeply vested interests in lies. We say to the daughter, "You can talk about the abuse you experienced from your stepfather." We say to tobacco companies, "We know you are advertising to our children and that is wrong."

Writers and therapists live twice—first when they experience events and a second time when they use them in their work. Writers and therapists face worthy opponents. Writers call it the inner critic or writer's block. For therapists it is resistance. We can only be successful when we learn to confront and conquer that opponent.

Both therapists and writers work at the edge of our envelopes. Faulkner wrote, "Writing a novel is like trying to knock together a chicken coop in the middle of a hurricane." Somerset Maugham observed, "There are three secrets to writing a novel. Unfortunately no one knows what they are."

Our work as therapists is complex and ambiguous. Success remains elusive and temporary. Writers must continually fight our awareness that we are not smart enough or skilled enough to do what we want to do. Therapists constantly discover that we simply aren't capable of changing human beings. Both jobs are frustrating, demanding, and fraught with emotional peril, and they are the best jobs around. As William Stafford said, "It's really fun if you can stand it."

Many therapists speak of their gratitude that they are allowed the honor of doing the work they do. And over the years I have never met anyone who said she was sorry she was a writer. Both kinds of work share great rewards—lives lived intensely and fully, and conversations that are close to the heart of matters. We're damn lucky we have this work.

Laura, I hope sometime you can visit Capetown. I'll leave here with my heart aching and my mind churning. In Langa, women washed their clothes by hand at a lone water pump, and sheep heads covered with flies were piled on street corners, meat for the poor in that sad place. And yet, the jacaranda trees rained purple flowers. Another tree, called the yesterday, today, and tomorrow tree, blossomed in three colors, white, pink, and red. Now that's an image a poet or therapist could turn into a metaphor.

▪ PART IV: FALL

21
■ Ethics

Dear Laura,

Let me tell you the story about an unlicensed therapist who wreaked havoc in my hometown. This smarmy guy found a lonely rich woman, and he scheduled several hour-long sessions a day with her, seven days a week. Alone in his office with the woman and her checkbook, he managed to seduce her and bilk her of her fortune. Then when she was broke, he abandoned her. She responded by swallowing a bottle of sleeping pills and had a mental breakdown. Her relatives, left to deal with the fallout of her collapse and her newfound poverty, reported the therapist to the health department. As quickly as he blew into town, he blew back out. By now, no doubt, he is defrauding clients in another state.

Thank goodness there are not many stories as bad as this one. This guy was not just unethical, he was criminal. For the most part, psychologists who land in ethical "hot water" fall into three categories; greedy manipulators (mercifully few), inadequate people whose therapy clients are their only relationships (not many of these either), and isolated or burned-out therapists who lose perspective (the largest group). Fortunately, psychology has the Code of Ethics to protect us and our clients. Some of the time the code and a few guidelines are sufficient. Hippocrates's famous dictum, "Physician, do no harm," applies to many situations as does my mother's goodbye advice to us kids, "Be kind to each other."

In clinical practice as in life, there are many problems that these simple guidelines don't address. I am conflicted about using and sharing diagnoses with clients, insurance companies, or institutions. Diagnoses are still reasonably subjective. But even when the evidence for a diagnosis is compelling, I am uneasy about labeling anyone unless I can see that the benefits will outweigh the costs.

I worked with a boy who could probably have been labeled as having obsessive compulsive disorder. Oliver washed his hands so often they were chaffed and he insisted that every object he owned be in its right place. He worried far too much about his homework and his haircuts. Diagnosing Oliver might have qualified him for extra services at school. But I worried how the label might affect his own and other's view of him. Finally, I decided we could help Oliver without labeling him. His parents and I could discuss how to distract him from his ruminations. His family doctor could write a prescription if necessary. None of this required that we officially diagnose Oliver.

We can't anticipate all of the events that a label may trigger. Diagnoses give and they taketh away. They lead us into and out of swamps. Before we diagnose, ask ourselves, "Why are we doing this? Will a diagnosis allow clients to get the help they need? Can the diagnosis hurt the client?"

Another ethical issue concerns the difference between understanding and approval. After I have seen clients for a while, I find it easy to understand why they act as they do. But I must work to not confuse understanding with condoning. Sometimes the distinction is crystal clear. An abused child may torment animals or set fires—understandable behaviors, but terrible ones. I can care for the child, but dislike his behavior. Other times it is harder. A man raised by cold parents repeatedly seduces women, then abandons them. I must make sure my knowledge of his history doesn't cloud my awareness that his attachment issues are someone else's heartbreak.

This separation of understanding and judgment requires a certain mental finesse. Racists are an example of this thorny problem. The worst racist I ever worked with came from a hateful, abusive family. I felt great sympathy for the man, who in some ways was much kinder than his parents. He sobbed in my office at the thought that his wife might leave him and take the children. But he was a member of a white supremacy group and somehow I had to deal with that fact. Finally I told him that I couldn't work with him if he remained with this group. I so deeply rejected his ideology that it damaged our relationship. He left without paying and never returned.

Another client wanted help dealing with the stress of her affair with a married man. Her goal was to convince this wealthy man to leave his wife and three kids and marry her. I told her that I didn't help clients reach goals that I believed would harm them or other people.

I worked with a woman who dealt with all her sadness and anger by shopping. This woman was depressed, but not about shopping, which was her one pleasure in life. I made it a personal goal to steer this client toward volunteer work, walks, and good books.

Laura, I don't tell you these stories to illustrate my exemplary work. In fact, in all these examples, I am not sure I even did the right thing. The white supremacist left therapy angrier than when he came in. The gold digger eventually married the rich man, and I now see them almost weekly at the movies, the grocery store, or in cafés. Very awkward! The shopping client didn't like to walk on anything but pavement and she preferred playing the lottery to reading Willa Cather.

I tell you these stories to show that my values influenced my work. Over the years many of my clients ended up back in college, playing classical music, or doing volunteer work, all activities I value highly. In spite of what some theorists suggest, we can't claim to be and we shouldn't be value neutral. Our responsibility is to be honest with our clients about our values.

Therapists are sometimes naïve about evil. I remember one therapist who dated a convicted murderer recently released from our state prison. He was clearly a jerk, interested only in her body and her apartment, but she claimed she could see the good in him. Well maybe. . . but I felt she was so nonjudgmental as to have virtually no common sense.

Compassion is only useful when coupled with clear-headedness. Being big-hearted and fuzzy-minded can get us in trouble. One of our ethical responsibilities is to evaluate who has the likelihood of harming others and to take steps to protect potential victims. If we suspect a man might assault his girlfriend, we have a duty to warn her. If we know an adolescent is shooting up heroin, we need to tell his parents and find him treatment.

Finally, we have an ethical responsibility to know that we don't know everything. Every heart is a mystery, but some mysteries are harder to fathom than others. It can be a stretch for middle-class whites to understand the issues of African-Americans, the disabled, refugees, or the poor. Unless we make a real effort to learn about the environments that our clients experience, our advice is likely to be ridiculous.

Older clients humble me. I am a long way from age eighty and I can't imagine what it feels like. It seems presumptuous to give advice to someone who has had many life experiences I haven't encountered. How would I know how to cope with the loss of my mate, my siblings, my friends, and my home? Yet I have seen, and you will see, many older clients. And amazingly, sometimes we actually help them.

With the exception of the fly-by-night, low-life snake-oil salesperson, or the seriously misinformed, nobody becomes a therapist to get rich. Therapists make enough money, though, and, in a way, I'm glad we don't make more. If we did, we'd attract more rotten apples to our profession. Almost all of us are in this work because we want to help. We like people and they like us back.

22
■ Story Doctors

September 21

Dear Laura,

On this day in 1944, my parents married in a red-wood forest in Mill Valley, California. They wore their military uniforms. The sun was shining and afterward they went with their friends to an Armenian restaurant on Geary Street in San Francisco. They had met in that beautiful city when Avis was an officer and Frank a seaman second-class assigned to shine officer's shoes. Both were good-looking, energetic, and adventurous. As my dad put it, "We'd try anything once." Their courtship was a dramatic tale, sometimes funny, but in retrospect, poignant and filled with foreshadowing of their future troubles as husband and wife.

My folks have been dead for many years, but I am grateful that my mother was a storyteller. As I rode along with her on house calls and to hospitals, she told me hundreds of stories. Fifty-eight years after the newlyweds stood under a redwood and said their vows, my parents shimmer in my memory.

Yesterday, I ran into an old client of mine at the grocery store. Hal was wearing a shirt with a logo designed to look collegiate, only his college was Euphoric State. That made me smile because, years ago, Hal had come to see me with depression. He was a truck driver with a dull, solitary life. I couldn't figure out how to help him until I asked questions about his past: "What do you know about your birth? Were you a wanted child? What were you like as a young boy? How did you handle your first day of school?" Hal had no answers to those questions. When I asked about family vacations, he answered, "We never took one." When I inquired about family friends, he said, "My folks kept to themselves." I asked about hobbies and interests and Hal shook his head. Hal had almost no memories from his childhood or stories of his adult life. In fact, Hal had only one story. He was a sad, bored bachelor.

Hal's folks lived isolated, suspicious lives. His dad had been nicknamed Lumpy for reasons no one remembered, but which I suspected related to lack of charisma and low energy level. Lumpy prohibited talk at meals or while he was driving. When Hal spoke up, his dad would reply by saying, "Who do you think you are?" Or, "If you think you're so damn smart. . . ." Hal quickly learned not to volunteer information. Hal's mom kept to herself. She clearly didn't think she was so smart. His sister was much older than Hal and married when she was sixteen. After dinner Lumpy worked in his shop and Eva read *True Romance* or crocheted silently in her bedroom. The loudest sound in the house was the grandfather clock that chimed every fifteen minutes. Hal said, "I liked that clock."

We couldn't redo Hal's childhood, but we could reconstruct it. I helped him discover old stories and invent new ones for himself. His parents were dead, but I instructed him to call his sister and his aunt and ask for help filling in what I dubbed "the missing years." He wrote down their memories and we embellished them. For example, his sister remembered how much he liked baking day. His mom and aunt would bake Swedish rye bread on Saturdays. Hal would slather a warm chunk with butter and cinnamon sugar and go sit out back in the maple tree to eat it. His aunt remembered him as always hungry. We made these slivers of memories into a life theme—he'd always had a deep appreciation for the flavor of life. He'd always been hungry for adventures and for human connections. And he still had that deep hunger, which he was now ready to satisfy.

I gave Hal the assignment to bring in adventures from his current life every week. Hal doubted he could do this, but not surprisingly, when he started looking for stories he found them. When he shared them with me, I encouraged him to recall significant details and sparkling moments. I asked about the meaning of events, such as running into an old classmate or helping an older lady with a flat tire. As we talked, these memories expanded. The high school classmate, who had been happy to see him, allowed Hal to reevaluate some of his school experience as positive. The flat tire incident became a story about his big heart and the rewards of helping others.

There is a big difference between people who've had interesting lives and people who are interesting. That difference is storytelling. Events alone are not particularly compelling. Story illuminates motive, desire, and the complexities of the human heart. Just as good stories create healthy people and cultures, sick stories yield dispirited people and cultures.

We therapists are primarily storytellers. Most clients need stories that allow them to view the world in more optimistic ways. Therapist Jay Haley encouraged therapists to help their clients conceptualize themselves as heroes of epics. He spoke of "turning tragedy into musical comedy." Better stories allow our clients to see themselves as more heroic, passionate, and interesting.

Once I saw a grandmother burdened with the care of her cocaine-addicted son's child. Miriam was whipped when she came in—depressed, low-energy, and overwhelmed by her burdens. She saw her future as unending drudgery and herself as drab and pitiable. Crying throughout the first session, she said, "I don't think you can help. Even God couldn't help me." Since she was a strong Catholic, I thought she might be receptive to a Mother Teresa comparison. I told her that her mission was to help the small and weak. Care of her grandson was important and noble work. I said, "You can be proud that when duty called, you came running." That comparison didn't take the dirty diapers and crying baby away, but it gave Miriam a sense of honor. She agreed to return and, when she did, we looked for resources for her. I said, "Even Mother Teresa had a support system."

Many couples need new stories. Argumentative relationships can be reframed as passionate. We can compare their turbulence to that of more glamorous couples, such as Madonna and Guy Ritchie or Katherine and Petruchio from *The Taming of the Shrew*. At the same time we can suggest that our clients have the stability to harness all that energy and turn it into sustained passion.

Refugees often construct new stories. They come to America with memories of victimhood. I ask them what they can recall with pride. Often they remember acts of courage or generosity. Small changes in their stories can have big implications for identity. A young woman from Bosnia remembers that she protected her sister from being raped by pushing her behind a door when the soldiers came. This memory allows her to feel noble instead of just soiled. All is not a wasteland. Amongst the rubble we can help our clients find buried treasure.

As Isak Dinesen said, "All sorrows can be borne if they are put in a story." We can help make our client's narratives richer, more complex, and hopeful. The most common way to do that is to respond to any sad story with the question—"What did you gain from this experience?" Amazingly I have never had a client who didn't gain something.

I am proud to report that when I ran into Hal in the produce section, he told me a story. It wasn't the best story I've ever heard. He's no Studs Terkel. But it was a real story, about a trip he took with his girlfriend to Yellowstone National Park. A bear broke into their car and ate their provisions. Hal chased it away. He was loved in the story and he was a hero. Indeed Hal's "Euphoric State" T-shirt reflected a new reality for him.

My parents didn't live happily ever after; they lived turbulently ever after, rather like Katherine and Petruchio. But they were both storytellers and because of that I experienced a rich childhood. Very little happens in my adult life that doesn't remind me of a story I heard as a girl. Sometime this fall during supervision, Laura, let's put aside cases and just tell stories. They have kept us humans sane during long, dark seasons for many generations.

23
■ Resistance

October 4

Dear Laura,

Iraqis have a saying: "You can wake up a sleeping dog, but not one who is pretending to be asleep." This morning's paper featured a picture of Emma, who I'd seen as a sullen, recalcitrant teenager. She was a PK, a preacher's kid, whose parents brought her in because she wouldn't eat meals with the family. Emma has just graduated at the top of her law-school class. I chuckled to think that now she was utilizing the debating skills she'd honed on me and on her parents.

At Emma's first session, she stared out my window with her arms crossed over her chest. When I said I hated to waste my time and her parents' money, she quipped, "Cry me a river." She began talking only after I mentioned how restful she was after all my talkative clients. Then she talked nonstop. The problem was that she didn't listen. So I listened. I looked for ways into her world, for metaphors that might touch her, and new ways to frame her situation. I waited for her to ask for my opinion and, after a few sessions, she did. She yawned theatrically while I answered, but she actually followed some of my suggestions.

I always let Emma have the last word, an important skill in dealing with stubbornness. Once she'd taken her best shot, she would calm down and be less defensive. Then during that grace period, I could sneak in a small point. We waltzed this way for many months. She never really embraced therapy, but as long as no one tried to make her admit it, she made some progress. By the time Emma terminated, she was sharing meals with her family.

Psychologist Carl Rogers spoke of the paradox of change—that people only seriously consider change when they feel accepted for exactly who they are. Resistance to change is a natural part of the human condition. Whenever I hear someone described as "not taking criticism well," I want to ask, "Who does take criticism well?"

We all want progress, but we don't like change, especially change imposed from the outside. No matter how crushing our problems, we generally prefer them to uncertainty. And when push comes to shove, we don't want to trade our problems for the problems of anybody else. To a certain extent, we are our problems. To lose them is to lose our identity.

We therapists can lead a horse to water, but we can't make him write in his journal and exercise daily. The truth is, people do exactly what they want to do. Our biggest challenge is helping people want to do what's in their best interest. You have heard the old joke. "How many therapists does it take to change a light bulb? One, if the light bulb wants to change." Education, example, support, and exhortation all work, if the client sincerely wants to change.

People may come to therapy because they are afraid of losing someone they love, but often they don't want to work all that hard. In fact, reluctant clients may use the therapy as a tool to get people off their backs. "Hey, don't bug me about my drinking. I'm working on it in therapy." More often, people change in response to love. Many a parent has quit smoking when her kindergartner begged her to. Many an adolescent has settled down when his grandparents took him on a fishing trip.

It's impossible to stop a roaring river, but you can change a river's flow by digging a small ditch or building a small dam. It's almost always better to deflect resistance than to meet it head on. There are many ways to do this. One is to say something like, "I agree with part of what you are saying, but there is a small part I wonder about," or even better, "I wonder if you have even the slightest doubts about your current position." Or, "I can see you dislike what I am suggesting, but I wonder if you would consider trying it for a few days."

You can tell a story about a person similar to your client who did things just a little bit differently. Or, you can discuss the advantages for a person not to change, and hope your clients will argue with you. When clients ask me if they have time to solve a problem, my favorite answer is, "You have just enough time."

There are two rules for power struggles—avoid them or win them. In therapy, they are almost impossible to win. After all, clients are in charge of their own lives. But often power struggles can be won indirectly. When I worked with Lynn, a shy woman who rarely had fun, I encouraged her to exercise. No way, she would argue. Lynn had a hundred reasons why she couldn't exercise even five minutes a week. Finally, I suggested a dog. My thinking was threefold. It would give Lynn an attachment, always curative with depression. It would also provide her with a topic of conversation, something that would help her "get started" with other people. And, walking her dog, Lynn would crank out a few endorphins.

Lynn agreed to adopt a dog, not for my reasons, but for her personal safety. Duke was a big dog who loved to romp outdoors. Soon Lynn was going farther and farther each day. Racing after Duke gave her enough exercise and excitement that she didn't need medication. In addition, she visited with dog owners on the trail and she maintained a constant supply of Duke stories for her coworkers.

Motivating others involves an almost mystical state of being "in tune" with them. This is called by names such as "being in sync" or "clicking." We all know it when we feel it. Scientists have a term, "limbic resonance," that refers to the innate ability of mammals to sense each other's emotional states. Change is most likely to occur when we sense that the people with us are attentive and accepting. When we feel that, we are more open to new experiences. Composer Benjamin Zander says he knows when people click with him because they have "shining eyes." Those shining eyes are good signs you have connected with your clients.

Often people come to us when they are ready to change. Timing is everything. If a suggestion is timed properly, it can be very small and still change a life. If improperly timed, a thunderbolt won't do much. The art of therapy is to be just a tad ahead of clients, to be ready with a remark that makes the client say, "That's just what I was thinking."

Poorly timed interventions can be worse than none at all because they ruin the potential for later attempts and they inspire a great deal of resistance. For example, I erred in suggesting that Lynn attend a single-adults' meeting at a church. She didn't have the social skills or the confidence for that event and suffered an embarrassing evening. Never again was I able to persuade her to take that kind of risk.

Often a way to know that our timing is off is when we find ourselves not wanting to say something. Most likely, we are sensing that the client is not ready to hear what we have to say. Usually ignoring our own sense of resistance is a bad idea. One exception to this is addictions. People who are hooked almost never want to discuss their habits, and sometimes it's too dangerous to wait until they are ready. However, when I find myself explaining too much, repeating, or arguing with clients, I know I have hit a wall and I won't be breaking it down.

When clients don't change, we may think to ourselves, "What? You're not taking my brilliant, carefully considered, expertly delivered advice?" But life is always more complex than that. Emma's behavior toward me wasn't about me. Personalizing resistance just makes it harder to overcome. Laura, use resistance to gather information about yourself and your clients. The only way you can truly avoid resistance is to stay home from work.

24
▨ Failures

Dear Laura,

You are being too hard on yourself. Missing an important theme in a discussion is not an irreparable mistake. Important material circulates over and over. You will catch it next time.

In the ideal case, a client comes in with a problem, and the therapist and the client develop a respectful, caring relationship. They solve the immediate problem and perhaps explore other aspects of the client's life. Then the client terminates with an evaluation of the therapy and feedback for the therapist on what was helpful. The therapist uses that last session to solidify gains, discuss potential problems and victories, and to praise the client for genuine growth. This best-case scenario doesn't happen all that often.

You asked me once, "What about your failures? What were your worst mistakes?" I have avoided answering you until today. It's painful and a little humiliating to admit defeats. I've never had a client commit suicide or assault anyone during our work, but a few of my screw-ups have been doozies.

Some failures were predictable. I've often been unable to help chaotic families with deeply entrenched problems, especially if they rarely showed up for appointments. Sadly, I never figured out how to help character disorders, which is our academic way of describing people without consciences. For a while I saw a man who cheated, charmed, and fornicated his way through life. Norm's character structure was set in cement and I was just another person to hoodwink. Eventually Norm's business failed because of his corrupt practices, but his long-suffering wife chose to stick it out. "Time wounds all heels," but it wounds their families, too. With my conversations and assignments, I wasn't of much help to Norm or his wife.

Other failures were a surprise—clients who seemed reasonable, engaged in the process, and meeting their goals would suddenly drop out or sabotage the therapy in ways that wrested defeat from the jaws of victory.

If the deck was stacked against therapeutic success from the beginning, I did only a brief postmortem. I asked myself, "What could I have done differently? What did I miss?" Then I'd move on without much more soul searching. However, if I had held high hopes for the therapy, I would feel pretty stung. Usually, I would try to convince the client to come in for one last session to talk over our difficulties. I would replay the therapy with my office partners and ask for alternative approaches. I would toss and turn for nights, reflecting on my own stupidity.

In retrospect, some mistakes were obvious. I had a long-term therapeutic relationship with a gentle mother of three who appeared stable, hard working, and happily married. Hannah had been a teenage alcoholic, but she had achieved sobriety through Alcoholics Anonymous. In her twenties she stole prescription drugs from the pharmacy where she worked. She was fired but not arrested. When I saw her in her thirties, she claimed to be drug free. The puzzle was that, as a therapy client, she reported almost no problems at all. She chatted amiably about parenting and small tensions with her husband or coworkers. Occasionally I asked her if she was drinking or doing drugs and she adamantly denied it. But one Tuesday, three hours after an appointment, Hannah was arrested for possession of cocaine.

I should have viewed Hannah's lack of problems as a red flag. Busy working people don't pay ninety bucks an hour to chat. I should have been in better contact with her husband, who later told me, "Hannah's been weirder than hell. I had my suspicions." I should have exercised my hate-it-but-do-it muscle and required regular drug screens. Hannah was sweet and I was polite. But all that nicey-nice time landed her in prison and cost her a marriage.

I worked with a bulimic client named Rosemary for three years. I tried everything with her—in-depth discussions of her past, feelings journals, food diaries, assertiveness training, stress management, cognitive-behavioral therapy, and finally even inpatient treatment. Rosemary made no progress and after a year I, the author of a book on eating disorders, passed her on to a new therapist. Something she said in our last session made it clear what had gone awry. Rosemary said, "I am sorry you couldn't find the right way to help me." I realized she saw me as possessing an infinite bag of tricks from which I would eventually pull a cure. She was waiting for my magic to arrive. I should have said, "I'm not a wizard. Only you can fix things."

One of my saddest cases was a teenage boy whose father killed himself in a drunk driving accident. After the funeral, Brandon came in with his mother. The two of them fought constantly. Brandon ran away from home, yelled at his mom, and stole from her. At one point, I suggested that perhaps Brandon should move into a group home where there would be more control. The mother and son never returned to therapy. When I analyzed what had happened, I gave myself a well deserved kick in the pants. These two traumatized people only had each other. Their fighting was a way to stay connected and diverted from their pain. I was a fool to think of separating them.

Other cases were harder to second-guess. I saw a woman named Moira who never stopped talking. I tried to wait her out. I thought that perhaps, for reasons I didn't understand, she needed the floor 100 percent of the time. As time passed, I attempted to confront Moira about her volubility, but I couldn't get a word in edgewise. She was terrified to come up for air and listen to me or anyone else. She may well have had what Melanie Klein called the "manic defense," which is basically an attempt to outrun depression by never slowing down to think. Once I actually suggested this to her, but Moira didn't pause long enough to consider the idea. Mercifully for me, Moira eventually stopped coming in for her gabfests. Neither she nor I felt she'd made any progress. In the end, I don't think she wanted help. She wanted praise. But even for compliments, she wouldn't stop talking.

After all these years, writing about my mistakes causes my stomach to hurt. I don't like to fail and I'm not one to easily let go. But it's more than that. I worry I hurt people who came to me for help. I regret I couldn't manage to find keys to unlock intractable clients' resistance. As I said, I'm not one to easily let things go.

An art teacher I respect doesn't allow her class to use erasers in their drawings. She says, "Don't erase a mistake, make it beautiful." After a rambling, unproductive session, I could often save something at the end. I might say to my client, "Sometimes after a murky session, clients will have a revelation on the way home that really clarifies our discussion." Or, "We touched on many subjects today. The results are not yet visible to us, but we have begun an irreversible process." These cryptic remarks kept clients searching for meaning until we met again. Often when we did, they would have discovered something luminescent in that drab previous hour.

As a parent, a therapist, and a writer, I am on target maybe 70 percent of the time. To expect more of myself would be expecting more perfection than a mere middle-aged mortal can muster. I remember my Uncle Otis's advice. On his sixtieth wedding anniversary, a party guest asked for his words of wisdom. Otis was embarrassed by the request but took his duty seriously. He said, "I try to get a good night's sleep and get up every morning and do the best that I can."

25
▉ Healing Solutions from All Over the World

October 21

Dear Laura,

Last night Jim and I drove into the country during sunset. It was harvest and all the grain dust in the air made the sun look like a persimmon. Our state smelled like a big box of cereal. Lights blinked and bobbed in the fields and old trucks waited in long lines by the Walton elevator. Fifteen-feet-tall sunflowers nodded in the ditches. The coats of horses gleamed in the slanted light.

All over the world humans imbue the sunset with meaning. Other totemic objects are plants or animals that are different from the norm. Nature's aberrations are worshipped or feared. For a year, we had an albino squirrel in our neighborhood. Whenever I happened to see him, I felt a burst of pleasure, followed by other feelings: hope, serenity, and even awe. He disappeared, no doubt devoured by a predator, and I still look at the place he used to scamper. The Plains Indians revered the white buffalo. They believed that when a white calf was born good fortune would come to the people. And I just read in the *New Yorker* about the incredible golden spruce that lived on the Queen Charlotte Islands off British Columbia. Tourists, residents of the island today, and the Haida Indians worshipped this tree. A man cut it down in a terrible act of vandalism. But even he must have felt it was sacred, sacred enough to destroy for symbolic reasons.

All cultures have systems of healing. Universal treatments include good food, music, touch, truth-telling, and forgiveness. Many Native-American cultures have talking circles where adults sit together and tell stories about whatever issues need discussed. Drums, drinks, and the burning of aromatic plants all serve to cure many ills.

In many places, people enact purification and forgiveness rituals. Talking to friends, enjoying children, and creating art are ways of healing that have been used for millenniums. Laughter is a part of many healing systems. There is an Iraqi saying, "Three things are calming—grass, water, and the face of a beautiful woman." Bosnians say, "There is a bond between the heart and grass."

In the Middle East, troubled people often visit saints' houses. Usually these are peaceful retreats staffed by kind people who assist the travelers. Guests visit with each other and share food. They pray, cry, walk, and rest. Most return home feeling much better.

Buddhism has an ancient and sophisticated set of practices for calming and healing. Breathing properly, meditating, and focusing on the impermanence of all things are healing activities. Some of our most successful psychotherapy incorporates aspects of Buddhism.

Victims of repressive governments sometimes repair psychic damage by documenting the abuses of an authoritarian regime or working for human rights. Bringing family over from the old country is profoundly healing. Once I asked a Sudanese man what would help him heal from all the deaths he had experienced. He said, "I want to be with my people. When I can help them, I am happy."

Traditional healers and customs work because they are believed to work. Almost all mental health cures involve placebo effects. In therapy people improve partly because they expect to improve. They count on what a Vietnamese boy I met at a high school described as, "The beauty and mystery of hope."

Praying works whether or not people believe in God. Prayer is a more active, trusting process than worrying. Most people find talking to God more satisfying than talking to Freud. Also with prayer, there is no need for diagnosis, treatment, or comprehensive health insurance.

Attention is curative. People feel better when they feel heard and when they feel loved. When a Hmong shaman puts on a horse-head mask and dances around a room chanting, his patient understands that someone is paying attention to him and that his family has carefully arranged and paid for this attention. Love regenerates dispirited and desperate people. As poet Joy Harjo wrote, "Love changes molecular structure."

Most refugees don't take to therapy as we practice it. Sitting in a small room with a stranger talking about problems is a pretty odd idea. Besides, they are focused on survival issues such as paying rent and getting shoes for their kids. Therapist Sara Alexander encourages refugee clients to design individualized "healing packages." These are plans to do certain things that will propel them into new lives. I knew a woman from Schrebrenica who had lost twenty-two men from her family in one day. She told me, "The pain has killed my heart." She rejected psychotherapy but was extremely pleased by free tickets to the circus. Fun with her family was part of her healing package.

You will soon see clients who give you the opportunity to be less ethnocentric and Eurocentric. In this new century all of us will need universal methods of healing. We won't necessarily keep all the Western boundaries between mind and body, spiritual and worldly, and work and play. We'll assign our clients massages, walks in the woods, music, tai chi, and aroma therapy. We will write prescriptions for potlucks and dances.

26
■ Yearning

November 6, 2002

Dear Laura,

I was deeply touched last session to hear about the dreams of your new client. Since he was a boy, Andy has wanted to travel to Italy, to ride the ferry on Lake Como, and to hear an opera in Milan. You and I agreed that trip isn't in the near future for a man supporting a wife and three kids on a carpenter's salary. Andy reminds me of a fellow from my hometown who couldn't travel, but swore he had roamed the whole world by subscribing to *National Geographic*.

What yearners we humans are. In all times and places we have wanted more, more, more. We have wanted to be with people who were dead or far away, or to be in different places or times in our lives. We have yearned for richer harvests, warmer huts, or to be stronger or more beautiful. We've desired more family or less, more work or less, and more complexity or more simplicity. Long ago Basho, the Japanese master of haiku, wrote, "Even in Kyoto, hearing the cuckoos cry, I yearn for Kyoto."

This is especially true for Americans today, partly because advertising educates us to want more than we have, but also because we're flooded with more things to want. We can desire a DVD player, a trekking adventure in Nepal, a Lexus, or an MBA. Americans have grown richer over the course of the last century, but as our standard of living has risen, so have our expectations. The gap between what we want and what we possess has widened.

On almost all measures of mental and social health we've grown poorer. Right now the United States has one of the highest rates of depression in the world. When Mother Teresa visited America she noted that we have a worse poverty than India, a spiritual poverty, a loneliness that comes from wanting the wrong things.

Writing *The Middle of Everywhere*, I came to see our culture more clearly. We Americans often are ignorant about the world and indifferent to the plight of others. We were born on third base, thinking we had hit triples. Writing about refugees, I moved between two worlds— the America where people drank designer coffees and bought stereo systems and the America of hungry children and ramshackle houses. I'd listen to a friend complain that she couldn't find fresh basil, then I'd listen to a student cry as she told me her cousins in Ukraine were eating grass to stay alive. I would hear a colleague's report on his Alaskan cruise, then I'd visit a refugee family who reported that their relatives were starving in a camp in Ghana.

Recently I watched part of a "reality-television" program. I was disgusted and angered by it. Perhaps my work with refugees and the poor made me especially sensitive to its tastelessness. But I found it repugnant that in a world so filled with starving children and desperate people, Americans would watch manufactured trauma for entertainment. The superficiality and falsity of the show sickened me. If I had a choice of living with the creator of this show or living in the worst refugee camp in the world, I would choose the camp. At least there is something honest about suffering, about looking for food and shelter. Despair has a certain integrity.

For the most part, Americans born early last century had reasonable expectations. They came of age during the Depression when good luck meant you had shoes and dinner. But most Americans born after World War Two have been encouraged to believe we can have everything. Of course, this sets us up for misery. If happiness depends on the ratio of fulfilled desires to total desires, no person whose desires are infinite can be satisfied. In fact, long ago Tolstoy defined wealth as, "the number of things one can do without."

Research shows that there are basically two kinds of people, satisfizers and maximizers. Maximizers are people who always want to make the best choices. Satisfizers say, "Good enough." A satisfizer enjoys his meal at a restaurant. A maximizer asks himself, "Is this really the best place in town? And did I order the right dish?" Most human misery comes from having a 95 percent good life, but trying to achieve that last 5 percent.

We tend to discover what we seek. People who want money tend to acquire it. People who seek hedonistic pleasures, adventures, or love generally find what they want. People who look for humor find it, as do people who look for trouble. People are pretty much as happy as they make up their minds to be. As my Aunt Grace said from her rocking chair by the window where she watched birds feed, "I get what I want but I know what to want."

If our clients want to be rock stars, rear perfect children, or inhabit marriages filled with nonstop romance, they are doomed to fail. If they expect stress-free jobs or kids who don't sass, they are programmed for discontent. Contentment involves learning to balance one's dreams with reasonable expectations.

The opposite of yearning is savoring the exquisite now. As one yoga teacher called out in class, "Experience your body. Are you remembering it or feeling it?" We therapists can remind our clients of an equivalent message, "Be here now."

We can ask clients to keep a daily record of what they have appreciated. Gratitude rituals, such as saying grace or thanking others for small kindnesses, make a difference. A good way to fall asleep at night is to think back on all the pleasant events of the day. Counting blessings is good for mental health. Often I encourage couples to enter a compliment competition, to see which spouse can praise the other the most in a genuine way.

If we view lives as time lines, most people have both happy and sad eras. Especially toward the end, some years are rough. My life has been mostly lucky. As a child, I had a family filled with lively, good-hearted, if sometimes hapless, people. I have had a good education, challenging work, good health, and my own family to love. As an adult, I have had friends, adventures, and a home in a safe, quiet place. But my life, like everyone else's, has also been filled with sadness.

My parents both died long and agonizing deaths by inches. One of my closest friends committed suicide, another died of a brain tumor. I have worried a great deal about my work, my siblings, and my kids. I have endured chronic insomnia, surely one of life's greatest curses, and I have often felt anxious and inadequate for the tasks at hand. Like most writers, I am lonely. Sometimes I feel discouraged. I think of the ways I have failed and life has failed me, and I try to tell myself, "You have had a lot. Nobody gets everything."

Laura, right now Andy is in no position to go to Italy, but there may be a time when he can. Meanwhile, his dreams comfort him. Dreams have kept many people sane as they worked at boring jobs or coped with difficult times. Every now and then in the therapy you can bring up Italy. When Andy is discouraged with his life, you can ask him to describe what it might be like to ride in a gondola at night or drink wine at a small café near La Scala.

Fall is really the season of yearning. At the same time we're aware of the earth's fiery glory, we're aware of its passing and the approaching winter. We yearn to stop time, to make our lives an endless Indian summer. But the message of autumn is to accept what is given. What's coming next may be harder. As Ezra Pound wrote, "Winter is a-coming, sing god damn, sing god damn."

27

Things Are Becoming Something Else

November 23

Dear Laura,

I am getting ready for Thanksgiving. My kids will all be home. We'll have our usual walks on the prairie, Trivial Pursuit games, and movies. It is my favorite holiday— a celebration of family, even though we'll also have our usual arguments and tense moments. Then they will go home and winter will come.

After the holidays you'll have a new supervisor. I will miss your friendly smile and eager questions. I will miss writing you these letters.

Life is always changing. Time passes. Thoughts and emotions come and go. Tragedy strikes and then grace and joy peek around the corner. Relationships flourish and wither. Passion waxes and wanes. Hope flags and then returns at our darkest moment. Whatever is happening now will be replaced. The Buddhist concept of nonattachment is a helpful one.

In the end what I really want to say is this: Although many of us have joyous interludes, for most people life is hard. As author Wallace Stegner wrote, "We were going to leave our mark on life, but instead life left marks on us." Some lucky people enjoy delicious decades, but for many people every stage of life waxes at least as difficult as it is easy. Almost everyone I know has a much harder and more complicated life than others realize.

Parenthetically, this awareness allows me to tolerate cranks and grumps. When a clerk snaps at me, or a driver honks and gives me the finger, I tell myself, "Who knows what that person is enduring right now? Perhaps they have a family member dying, or are about to declare bankruptcy, or have just been dumped by the person they most desire."

Childhood is idyllic only in retrospect. Children have lives fully as complex as those of adults. Adolescence can be torture, young adulthood filled with angst, and adult life thorny with problems. People get married or they don't. Their children grow up or they don't. They grow ancient or they don't. Old age, if people make it that far, requires the patience of Job. To survive, we must all learn to live in the world with broken hearts.

My father's life is a case in point. He was born in 1916 in the Ozark Mountains. When he was young his father went crazy and was institutionalized for the rest of his life. My dad's family fell from status and wealth to shame-filled poverty. They lived in a cabin in the woods and ate squirrels and turtles, if they could catch them. During World War Two, as a medic in Okinawa and the Philippines, my father saw terrible things. All his adult life he struggled to find his place. He was Mr. Mom in an era when that role was seen as being a freeloader. He failed at a thousand get-rich-quick schemes. In the 1960s his teenagers let him down by becoming social activists. At fifty he had a debilitating stroke. Then he had many more strokes before dying, blind and crippled, at sixty-five.

Like many life stories, my father's was one of great sorrow, but also of great joy. My dad was good-looking, fun-loving, and popular. He was a high school basketball star. His mother and sisters doted on him and he married a woman he was crazy about who loved him until the end. He fished, traveled all over the world, and had a dozen hobbies. His story is no sadder than many others' lives. His life was a life.

In South Africa, I was enchanted by the Cape of Good Hope, the place where the icy, choppy Atlantic meets the serene and warmer Indian Ocean. That beautiful cape is also known as the Cape of Storms. In my mind I can see the cusp of a wave, the one that signals the place the Atlantic crashes into the Indian Ocean. The froth on that wave, that is where life is.

We are all more alike than we are different. In the end we all want the same things, what I called the five R's in my book *Another Country*. Beyond the basics such as food and shelter, but not really less essential, we all want respect, relaxation, relationships, results, and realization. Respect and relaxation are self-evident. By relationships, I mean we want to love and be loved. By results, I mean that we yearn to do good work. We want to live well and we need our lives to matter. Realization refers to fulfilling our potential. Margaret Mead defined the ideal society as one that has a place for every human gift. The ideal human life allows for the development of those gifts and their use for the benefit of others. Of course we all have our neuroses, our blind spots and our Achilles' heels. We're all Shakespearean buffoons as well as tragic heroes.

Yet, paradoxically, even as doing therapy has helped me see all of the cruelties and stupidities that we humans commit, it has also reinforced my belief, developed in my childhood, that most people are basically decent. I think of my client Helga, a middle-aged Czech woman who butchered hogs in her basement and called refrigerators "iceboxes" and garages "car sheds." She had been physically abused as a girl by her father and tormented during her years in school for being heavy and poor. She had married a farmer, much less intelligent than she, who had become very ill. Helga worked a factory job, ran the farm, and took university correspondence courses, even as she raised kids, cared for her husband, and did all the housework. She came to therapy because her husband, threatened by her intelligence, didn't want her to go to college. She felt she must complete her education so that she would be prepared herself to support the family when he was gone. And besides, she loved school. She pronounced the word "college," in a hushed and reverent way. As Helga and I talked, I felt what I often feel, a deep respect for the courage of ordinary people—the ones who get up every morning and do what needs to be done.

Therapists cannot eliminate sickness, death, bullies, financial scandals, mean-spirited coworkers, or unforgiving kin. But we are not helpless. We can tell people that, yes, life is hard, but they are not without adequate resources and wisdom to cope. We can spin a web of stories or help them make a careful decision. We can suggest they watch a sunset, cuddle a baby, or dance under cottonwoods. Buddha said, "Life is suffering," but he didn't say it was ignoble. At best, our work allows people to hallow suffering into empathy and wisdom.

We therapists are small potatoes, but we are connected to an ancient and beautiful idea. Since time began, humans have needed shamans, curanderos, and tribal healers. We have implored each other for help exorcising our demons. Since the beginning we have asked the same questions—Am I safe? Am I important? Am I forgiven? Am I loved?

Our profession has experienced its share of blunders, some of them disastrous. But our goals of understanding others' points of views, alleviating human suffering, and enhancing relationships are noble goals. At our best we respect the complexity of the universe with all its uproar and glory. Songwriter Greg Brown compared life to a "thump-ripe melon, so sweet and such a mess."

Writing this book I discovered that being a therapist is less about making a living and more about living my life. Simply put, it's a way of paying attention, which is the purest form of love. One of the Shavano Principles of Spiritual Activism is, "Do not insulate yourself from the pain of the world." The text reads, "When we open ourselves to the pain of the world, we become the medicine that heals the world."

Laura, there is no better work than the work we do. It has been a pleasure to watch you flower and bloom over the year. You will be an excellent therapist. Welcome to our field.

About the Author

Mary Pipher received her B.A. in cultural anthropology from the University of California at Berkeley in 1969, and her Ph.D. in clinical psychology from the University of Nebraska in 1977. Since then, she has explored cultural influences on mental health in five books, including best-sellers *The Shelter of Each Other*, *Another Country*, and the landmark *Reviving Ophelia: Saving the Selves of Adolescent Girls*, which spent 154 weeks on the *New York Times* best-seller list and has been translated into nineteen languages. Her most recent book, *The Middle of Everywhere: The World's Refugees Come to Our Town* (Harcourt, 2002), explores the effects of globalization on American society. Dr. Pipher has traveled all over the world lecturing to students, health care professionals, and community groups. She has been a psychotherapist in Nebraska since 1972.